SPIRIT-FILLED WORSHIP

Phil,
Let Every Breath
Praise the Lord!

2017

SPIRIT-FILLED WORSHIP

LEE ROY MARTIN

This is a pre-publication copy that has been printed for friends and family. The published edition, entitled

True Worship: Worship that Honors God, Strengthens the Church, and Impacts the World,

will be published soon in both English and Spanish and will be available from Senda de Vida Publishers, Miami, FL (305) 262-2627

This book is dedicated to
pastor Kevin Mendel
and the people of Grace Community Church

Lee Roy Martin holds the Doctor of Theology degree in Old Testament from the University of South Africa. He also has a B.A. in Biblical Studies from Lee University and a M.Div. from the Pentecostal Theological Seminary. In addition to his degrees, he completed three years of post-graduate study in biblical languages at Mid-America Baptist Theological Seminary. He has served 27 years as a pastor in the Church of God and now is Professor of Old Testament and Biblical Languages at the Pentecostal Theological Seminary in Cleveland, TN USA. He also serves as Editor of the *Journal of Pentecostal Theology*. He served as President of the Society for Pentecostal Studies, and he has taught Seminary extension courses at the Theological University of the Caribbean in Puerto Rico.

CONTENTS

CHAPTER 1

THE IMPORTANCE OF TRUE WORSHIP

You shall worship the LORD your God, and Him only you shall serve (Matthew 4:10).

A. Why should we study the topic of worship?

You may be wondering why you should study about worship and why you should read this book. We already know how to worship, right? Each of us has our own preferences regarding worship. We like to sing our favorite songs. We prefer to listen to our favorite preachers. We attend our favorite church. Why should we make time to read and study this book? For many reasons, I would suggest that the topic of worship is one of the most important topics that a Christian should study. Worship is to the spirit like breathing is to the body. Our worship of God is vital to the spiritual life of the individual believer and to the Church. This study of worship is needed for the following reasons.

1. Worship is a crucial topic in the world today

Worship is the most crucial issue for our time. The world is divided according to their object of worship and their methods of worship. In some religions, people worship their ancestors, but in other religions people worship various gods such as Buddha, Vishnu, Shiva, or Indra. The Muslims worship Allah, but Christians worship Jesus Christ. Hundreds and even thousands of people are fighting and dying because of their allegiance to the gods that they worship. Even within Christianity, the differences in worship have created conflict.

2. Worship is a crucial topic for the Church today

Worship is a crucial issue within the Church of today. People are asking how we should worship. Recent books suggest that the Church is currently experiencing a time of "worship wars," in which different visions of worship are competing against one another.[1] In addition to the significant distinctions between the worship of Roman Catholics and the worship of Protestants, we are also faced with differences between the liturgical Protestants (Anglican and Lutheran) and the non-liturgical Protestants of which Pentecostalism is a part.

Still further differences have developed within Pentecostalism itself, with newer congregations characterizing themselves as "seeker sensitive churches," "emergent churches," or "missional churches." What do these labels mean? How do these new perspectives affect our worship? These questions about overall perspectives of the Church lead to other questions that address specific worship practices: Should we sing only praise and worship songs to the exclusion of the old hymns? Is worship more effective when led by a praise team rather than a choir? Should we turn down the lights in the sanctuary so that the focus is on the platform? Should we hire professional musicians and singers? Are more people converted to Christ and filled with the Spirit in these new kinds of churches than in the more traditional Pentecostal churches? Should ministers invite people to pray in the altar on Sunday mornings? Should we discontinue Sunday evening worship services? How do we disciple our children and new converts? When and how will we provide an opportunity for people to be saved, sanctified, filled with the Holy Spirit, and healed? Should we allow the laity to exercise spiritual gifts such as tongues, interpretation of tongues, and prophecy? These are important questions for today's Church.

3. Worship is a crucial topic for contemporary life

Life has become more complicated than ever before, and people are occupied with many activities and with the accumulation of possessions. Jesus tells us that we cannot worship both God and money (Matthew 6:24), but many Christians are deceived by the

---

[1] The first of these books was Elmer L. Towns, *Putting an End to Worship Wars* (Nashville, TN: Broadman & Holman Publishers, 1997).

allure of riches. The apostle Paul warns us that covetousness is a form of idolatry (Colossians 3:5). Therefore, worship is a crucial issue in relation to the question of idolatry. Do we worship Jesus Christ, or have we made idols of our possessions: our cars, our homes, our jewels, our clothing, our bank accounts? Have we made an idol of our social standing, our status in the community? Have we made an idol of our work, our occupation? Have we made idols of sports heroes, movie stars, and other entertainers? The apostle Paul warns us that in the last days "perilous times" would come. Christians are commanded to love God with all of their hearts, but Paul says that the time would come when people would be "lovers of pleasure more than lovers of God" (2 Timothy 3:1-4). The book of Revelation warns that in the last days Christians will be tempted to worship materialism (Revelation 13:12-15), and the churches are commanded to repent and restore proper worship (Revelation 2:14-16; 20-22). Perhaps the Church should repent of its materialism.

4. Worship is a crucial topic in the Christian life

Worship is a crucial issue because worship is the most important activity in the Christian life. When Jesus Christ was tempted in the wilderness, the devil offered to Jesus "all the kingdoms" of the world if Jesus would only bow down and worship him (Matthew 4:9). But Jesus responded, "Away with you, Satan! For it is written, you shall worship the LORD your God, and him only you shall serve" (Matthew 4:10). We were created to live in a loving and faithful relationship with God, and our worship is one of the most powerful expressions of that relationship. We were created to worship God, our creator. Moreover, we were saved in order to become worshipers. We worship God because God is our savior. Our eternal destiny depends in part upon our faithful worship of God.

5. Worship is a crucial topic in relation to spirituality

Yes, worship is the most crucial issue of our time. It is not only important who we worship, but it is also important how we worship. Is worship only an obligation, a duty to perform, or is worship a joyful expression of our great love for our LORD and Savior? Is worship only to be endured, or should it be enjoyed? Is worship only a form and a ritual? Jesus Christ rebuked the Pharisees of his day by saying, "These people draw near to Me with their mouth, and honor Me with their lips, but their heart is far from Me" (Matthew 15:8). Furthermore, the apostle Paul warns us to "turn away" from people "having a form of godliness but denying its power" (2 Timothy 3:5). True worship, then, must be an offering of love to God.

6. Worship is a crucial topic for Pentecostalism

From Azusa Street until now, spiritual worship has characterized the Pentecostal movement. The Pentecostal revival has been key and influential in transforming the worship experience of the Church worldwide. Pentecostal worship has affected the worship experience of other denominations in positive ways. Furthermore, Pentecostal worship has spread around the world through the lives of 600 million faithful, worshiping, Pentecostal believers. Pentecostalism is the fastest growing Christian movement in the world, and this book is written with the hope that it will serve as a positive influence on the worship of this growing movement.

Unfortunately, the openness and exuberance of Pentecostal worship, the spontaneity, and the role of the congregation, have allowed at times for some unhealthy and unbiblical worship practices. Along with the fire, we sometimes find wildfire.

Genuine Pentecostal worship requires spiritual preparation and passion. That is, we should pray all during the week and seek for God's guidance for the worship services, and every participant should be prepared and be on time for the service. However, preparation is not enough to ensure spiritual worship. In addition to preparation, the church leaders and the congregation must have in their hearts a passion for God and a sensitivity to the leading of the Holy Spirit. The worship service, although planned and carefully organized, can be directed and redirected by the Holy Spirit. To be truly Pentecostal, worship must allow for the creative and innovative influence of the Holy Spirit. The apostle Paul tells us, "where the Spirit of the LORD is, there is liberty" (2 Corinthians 3:17).

The concerns mentioned above, along with many others, will be addressed throughout this book. I care deeply about worship, and I am committed to teaching the Body of Christ how to worship

God in the Spirit and in the Truth. It is that commitment and concern that gave birth to this volume, and while this brief study does not answer every question about worship, I hope that it will awaken the Church to the power and glory of worship.

B. The theological importance of worship

1. Worship is the heart of the biblical faith

What is the heart of Christianity? Is it our doctrines? Is it our church buildings? Is it our denominational structure? While all of these are vitally important, I do not see them as the heart of the Christian faith. The heart of our faith is our continual worship of Almighty God. The worship of God is the highest occupation of the Church, and worship fulfills the ultimate purpose for which the people of God are redeemed.

Many theologians would argue that doctrinal belief in the one true God is the heart of Christianity, but the apostle James writes, "You believe that there is one God. You do well. Even the demons believe – and tremble!" (James 2:19). Both the Christian and the demon believe in one God. The difference is that the Christian worships and serves God, but the demon does not.

Worship is essential to life. It is human nature to love and worship something; therefore, we will worship and serve either God or idols. We will worship something. We will love something. We will serve something. Worship is as natural as breathing (Psalm 150:6).

Worship is relevant and practically beneficial. The Church is the Body of Christ, and worship is the breath that fills the body with life and energy. Worship consumes our time, but it is well worth the investment. Without true worship, the Church is dead; however, when the Church worships God truly, it is the living embodiment of Christ in the world.

The psalmist David states that among all of the activities of life, the one most important is worship:

One thing I have desired of the LORD,
   That will I seek:

That I may dwell in the house of the LORD
  All the days of my life,
To behold the beauty of the LORD,
  And to inquire in His temple. (Psalm 27:4)

2. True worship is pleasing to God

Whenever we enter the House of God, we are tempted to enter with selfish motives. We may ask, "What can I get out of the experience?" We are tempted to think of worship as something that makes us feel good, something that meets our needs, something that will lift us up. However, the Bible indicates that worship should be aimed at God himself. Our worship should be a gift to God. It should be a gift that is pleasing to God. That is why the psalmist wrote these words:

The LORD takes pleasure in those who fear Him,
  In those who hope in His mercy (Psalm 147:11).

For the LORD takes pleasure in His people;
  He will beautify the humble with salvation (Psalm 149:4).

When the LORD takes pleasure in his people, he manifests himself and dwells in their praises (Psalm 22:3). When we worship God, we build a throne of praise, and we exalt the LORD so that he sits upon that throne. Our worship is an invitation for God to dwell among us in his glory and his majesty.

The pleasure of the LORD can become so great that he is moved to rejoice over us. The prophet Zephaniah penned these profound words:

The LORD your God in your midst,
  The Mighty One, will save;
He will rejoice over you with gladness,
  He will quiet you with His love,
  He will rejoice over you with singing (Zephaniah 3:17).

Consider how much God must love us! He is so happy with our worship that he rejoices over us, and he sings with joy.

God's enjoyment of our worship causes him to seek after worshipers. Jesus declares that "true worshipers will worship the Father in spirit and truth; for the Father is seeking such to worship

Him" (John 4:23). We will talk more later about what it means to worship in Spirit and in Truth. At this point, we should notice that God is "seeking" worshipers! God enjoys our worship. God takes pleasure in our worship; therefore, he searches for believers who will worship him.

3. Worship is an expression of our love for God

Worship is important because it is an expression of the believer's love for God. The first great commandment is "You shall love the LORD your God with all your heart, with all your soul, and with all your mind" (Matthew 22:37). Worship is one way that we demonstrate our love for God. If worship is not an act of love, then it is not pleasing to God. God is not pleased by worship that is motivated by a sense of duty and obligation alone. God desires worship that is willing and joyful.

4. Worship transforms us into the image of God

To use the words of pastor Tom Sterbens, worship is about "worth."[2] On the one hand, worship declares and celebrates the worth of God, the worthiness of God. The Ten Commandments forbids the making of idols, which is the forming or shaping of a god. The shaping of a false god is a shaping of its worth, which is not allowed. However, when we worship Jehovah God, we are forming and shaping the image of God through our praises and our words. Therefore, we are displaying God's worth.

On the other hand, worship declares and enhances our own worth as the people of God. Our worth is enhanced in worship in two ways. First, our character is displayed through the things that we value, honor, and worship. If we value money more than anything else, then our worth is tied to the amount of money that we possess. If we value and honor celebrities and sports heroes then our worth is tied to the success of those celebrities and sports figures. Our worship of God demonstrates that we value and honor God above all things. We cease our labors in order to make time for worship. We seek first the kingdom of God rather than seeking

---

[2] Tom Sterbens, "Worship: The Journey to Worth," in R. Keith Whitt and French L. Arrington (eds.), *Issues in Contemporary Pentecostalism* (Cleveland, TN: Pathway Press, 2012), pp. 185-210.

for all those things that the world seeks after. By devoting our valuable time, energy, and resources to the service and worship of Jehovah God, we shape our own character and worth. Our worth is shaped in a second way through worship – we become what we worship. There is an old proverb that says, "You are what you eat;" that is, whatever enters your stomach is digested and becomes a part of your body. In a similar way, whatever we consume with our minds and hearts becomes a part of our nature, behavior, and will. The more time that we spend in worship of God, the more we are formed and shaped into the image of God. The more we worship God, the more we become like God. Therefore, worship shapes our worth as we are transformed into the likeness of Jesus Christ "from glory to glory" (2 Corinthians 3:18).

C. The biblical importance of worship

The Bible is our most authoritative resource concerning worship practices. The importance of worship is emphasized throughout Holy Scripture in the following ways:

1. Worship is important because God has commanded us to worship him

God's people live in a committed covenant relationship to God, and worship is a vital element in that covenant relationship. The Israelites were commanded to worship God, and we should also consider these commands:

> but the LORD, who brought you up from the land of Egypt
> with great power and an outstretched arm, Him you shall fear,
> Him you shall worship, and to Him you shall offer sacrifice (2
> Kings 17:36).

> Give to the LORD the glory due His name;
>   Bring an offering, and come before Him.
> Oh, worship the LORD in the beauty of holiness!
>   (1 Chronicles 16:29)

> Sing praises to the LORD, who dwells in Zion! (Psalm 9:11)

> Be glad in the LORD and rejoice, you righteous;
>   And shout for joy, all you upright in heart! (Psalm 32:11).

Oh come, let us worship and bow down;
    Let us kneel before the LORD our Maker (Psalm 95:6).

Oh, worship the LORD in the beauty of holiness!
    Tremble before Him, all the earth (Psalm 96:9).

Exalt the LORD our God, and worship at His holy hill
                                        (Psalm 99:9).

Oh, give thanks to the LORD!
    Call upon His name (Psalm 105:1).

Praise the LORD! ...
Let everything that has breath praise the LORD.
Praise the LORD! (Psalm 150:1-6)

The New Testament also includes direct commands to worship:

You shall worship the LORD your God, and Him only you shall serve (Matthew 4:10).

Therefore, by Him let us continually offer the sacrifice of praise to God, that is, the fruit of *our* lips, giving thanks to His name (Hebrews 13:15).

Rejoice in the LORD always. Again I will say, rejoice! (Philippians 4:4)

Fear God and give glory to Him ... worship Him who made heaven and earth, the sea and springs of water (Revelation 14:7).

It is clear from these direct commands, that God wants his people to worship him. Surely, these directives from God should be enough to cause us to make worship our highest priority.

2. Worship existed before time itself

The Biblical story of worship begins before time itself. Worship is not something new. It is not something that we invented in the twenty-first century. The worship of God began even before humans were created. We read in the book of Job that before the earth was made, "the morning stars sang together, and all the sons of God shouted for joy" (Job 38:7). From the time they were formed, the seraphim have worshiped God with their continuous proclamation of "Holy, holy, holy is the LORD of Hosts" (Isaiah 6:3), and the cherubim have sung God's praises. Along with the seraphim and the cherubim, the angel Gabriel and the archangel Michael have worshiped before the throne of God.

3. All of creation exists to worship God

From the beginning of time, every created thing has fulfilled its purpose by worshiping God. All of creation exists for the ultimate purpose of giving glory and honor to the creator. Creation's adoration of God is expressed by the psalmist when he writes, "The heavens declare the glory of God; And the firmament shows His handiwork" (Psalm 19:1). The worship of all creation is elaborated further in Psalm 148:

Praise the LORD!
Praise the LORD from the heavens;
   Praise Him in the heights!
Praise Him, all His angels;
   Praise Him, all His hosts!
Praise Him, sun and moon;
   Praise Him, all you stars of light!
Praise Him, you heavens of heavens,
   And you waters above the heavens!
Let them praise the name of the LORD,
   For He commanded and they were created.
He also established them forever and ever;
   He made a decree which shall not pass away.
Praise the LORD from the earth,
   You great sea creatures and all the depths;
Fire and hail, snow and clouds;
   Stormy wind, fulfilling His word;
Mountains and all hills;
   Fruitful trees and all cedars;
Beasts and all cattle;
   Creeping things and flying fowl;
Kings of the earth and all peoples;
   Princes and all judges of the earth;
Both young men and maidens;

Old men and children.
Let them praise the name of the LORD,
     For His name alone is exalted;
     His glory *is* above the earth and heaven.
And He has exalted the horn of His people,
     The praise of all His saints –
     Of the children of Israel,
     A people near to Him.
Praise the LORD! (Psalm 148:1-14)

All of God's creation should praise him! This powerful praise should be given both to God the Father and to his Son Jesus Christ. The apostle Paul declares these powerful words of adoration regarding Jesus:

> He is the image of the invisible God, the firstborn over all creation. For by Him all things were created that are in heaven and that are on earth, visible and invisible, whether thrones or dominions or principalities or powers. All things were created through Him and for Him (Colossians 1:15-16).

All of creation was made "through" Jesus and "for" Jesus. This means that the purpose of creation is to give praise and honor to Jesus Christ. This view is supported by the vision of John, who reports the following in the book of Revelation:

> And every creature which is in heaven and on the earth and under the earth and such as are in the sea, and all that are in them, I heard saying:
>
> Blessing and honor and glory and power
>   Be to Him who sits on the throne,
> And to the Lamb, forever and ever! (Revelation 5:13)

Just as all of the heavenly hosts were created to worship God, so also humanity was created with the express purpose and destiny of worshiping God. After God had created the heavens and the earth, the sea and the dry land, the birds of the air, the fish of the sea, and the wild animals, God created humanity. God created Adam and Eve and placed them in a perfect environment that we call the Garden of Eden. God himself pronounced a blessing over his new creation, and he stated, "it is very good" (Genesis 1:31). The new creation was beautiful and harmonious.

Humanity was created in the image of God, and humanity was created with the ability to have fellowship with God. In all of our busy activities, it is easy for us to forget that our first priority should be fellowship with God. That is our created purpose.

God came down in the cool of the day to meet with Adam and Eve. They had fellowship with God that was completely unhindered by sin and unbelief. Adam and Eve enjoyed the presence of God, and God enjoyed the presence of Adam and Eve. Unfortunately, the perfect peace and harmony and joy of the garden of Eden did not last forever. When tempted by the serpent, Eve and then Adam disobeyed God, and their fellowship with God was forever radically hindered. The disobedience of Adam and Eve separated them from God's immediate presence. They were no longer able to visit with God face-to-face. They were no longer able to walk with God in the cool of the day. Very soon, all of humanity forgot the purpose of their existence. They forgot why they were created. They forgot how to worship God.

Even now, all of humanity that is outside of Jesus Christ has forgotten its reason for existence. People do not know their purpose in life. People do not know why they are created and what their goals should be. Ravi Zacharias, a well-known Christian speaker, writer, and apologist, states that our society has lost the answers to four crucial questions: 1. Regarding origin, Where did I come from? 2. Regarding meaning, Why am I here? 3. Regarding morality, How should I live? 4. Regarding destiny, Where am I headed?[3] These four questions are summarized ultimately in the question, "How and why am I here in the first place?"[4] If we go back to the beginning, and before the beginning, we will see that our purpose is the same as that of every other creation and of all of the host of heaven. We were created to worship God.

---

[3] Ravi K. Zacharias and Vince Vitale, *Jesus among Secular Gods: The Countercultural Claims of Christ* (New York: Faith Words/Hachette Book Group, 2017), p. 94.

[4] Zacharias and Vitale, *Jesus among Secular Gods*, p. 23.

This failure to understand our purpose has led to much dissatisfaction, confusion, broken relationships, social and cultural dysfunction, and a host of other ills. People want to know why they exist. People want to know if life has a purpose. The Bible has the answer to these concerns. We exist to serve God. Our lives have the purpose and the goal of worshiping God. If we are not worshiping God, then we are falling short of the reason for which we are created. Humans are the only earthly creatures who can freely choose to worship God. All creation praises God automatically through its ongoing display of God's glory. Humans, however, are made in the image of God, and we worship God by choice.[5]

4. Worship was prominent in God's covenant with Israel

The importance of worship is evident not only in the eternal worship of the heavenly hosts and in the deep fellowship of the first created humans in the garden of Eden, but also in the creation of God's people in the book of Exodus. The people of God had its beginnings in Genesis chapter 12 with God's call of Abraham. God promised to give descendants to Abraham and to make Abraham a mighty nation. Abraham responded to God's promises by perpetually worshiping God. In the book of Genesis, we read that everywhere Abraham traveled, he built an altar to the LORD.

At the end of the book of Genesis, the descendants of Abraham find themselves in the land of Egypt, where they have traveled to escape a famine in the land of Canaan. After a period of 400 years, the family of Abraham had become great in number, but they also had become slaves to their Egyptian hosts. They cried out to God for his help, and God remembered his covenant with Abraham. In Exodus 3, the LORD appeared to Moses in the burning bush, and he commanded Moses to go to Egypt and to deliver the Israelites out of Egypt. As soon as they were delivered from Egypt, they were to return to Mount Sinai and worship God there (Exodus 3:12).

---

[5] I offer my gratitude to my pastor, Kevin Mendel (MACM, MTS), for his sermons on worship and his insights regarding worship. Pastor Kevin's influence is evident here and at many other places throughout this book.

Therefore, the result of salvation is worship. The people of God are formed to a worshiping community. Some people do not understand this. They think that the church is here just for them to sit on the pew and watch someone else. The praise team worships. The choir worships. The pastor worships. Sometimes, the people in the congregation do not worship. But worship is for everyone, for all of God's people. Worship is important.

After they had been delivered from the Egyptian bondage, they returned to Mount Sinai to worship as the LORD had commanded. The LORD appeared to the Israelites in the form of fire, smoke, lightning, and darkness on the mountain. The LORD revealed his covenant to the people of Israel, and they agreed to serve the LORD faithfully. This covenant at Mount Sinai both began and concluded with instructions regarding worship. The heart of the covenant is the Ten Commandments, and those commandments begin with these words:

> I am the LORD your God, who brought you out of the land of Egypt, out of the house of bondage. You shall have no other gods before Me. You shall not make for yourself a carved image, or any likeness of anything that is in heaven above, or that is in the earth beneath, or that is in the water under the earth; you shall not bow down to them nor serve them. For I, the LORD your God, am a jealous God ... (Exodus 20:2-5).

These first two commandments specify that Jehovah God is to be Israel's only object of worship. Israel is forbidden to worship any other God, to create any carved images, or to serve any other God. God said, "I am Jehovah your God." When Jehovah says, "I am your God", he is claiming Israel for himself; and he is demanding their full and complete allegiance and devotion.

Not only does the covenant begin with instructions regarding worship, it also ends with instructions regarding worship. After the Ten Commandments and after various other commandments, Moses is given explicit and detailed instructions regarding the building of the tabernacle and the schedule for offering a variety of sacrifices. Israel had experienced God first through his promises to

Abraham and second through his deliverance of them out of bondage. Now, they will experience God through regular times of corporate worship at the tabernacle.

5. The Old Testament stresses the importance of worship
In addition to the specific instructions in the Sinai covenant, the Old Testament in general expresses the value of worship both to the individual believer and to the community of faith. Worship is so important that one entire book – the book of Psalms – is devoted to worship. The book of Psalms is the hymn book of Israel and of the early Church. The psalms are songs of worship that are sung in response to God's perfect character and to God's mighty acts. Whenever God acts, the appropriate human response is worship, as may be witnessed not only in the Psalms but also in other biblical texts where songs of praise and thanksgiving are recorded.

Returning to the story of Israel's salvation from Egyptian bondage, we observe a notable occasion of spontaneous worship. As soon as they realized that they were finally free from the Egyptians, and before they commenced their journey to Mount Sinai, the Israelites took time to worship God:

Then Moses and the children of Israel sang this song to the LORD, and spoke, saying:

I will sing to the LORD,
    For He has triumphed gloriously!
    The horse and its rider He has thrown into the sea!
The LORD is my strength and song,
    And He has become my salvation;
He is my God, and I will praise Him;
    My father's God, and I will exalt Him (Exodus 15:1-2).

After Moses finished singing his song, the worship continued:

Then Miriam the prophetess, the sister of Aaron, took the timbrel in her hand; and all the women went out after her with timbrels and with dances. And Miriam answered them:

Sing to the LORD,
    For He has triumphed gloriously!

> The horse and its rider
>> He has thrown into the sea! (Exodus 15:20-21).

The LORD delivered Israel from bondage; therefore, it was important to them that they make time for worship. Their worship was the proper response to God's mighty act of salvation. In the same way, we must make time for worship. Every day, God is with us; therefore, we should worship him. Every day, God answers prayers; therefore, we should worship him.

Worship is so important that Moses worshiped just before his death. The book of Deuteronomy consists of the last words of Moses, organized in the form of three sermons or speeches that he delivered to the Israelites while they were encamped at the edge of the Promised Land. When Moses finished his speeches and he had prepared to depart from this life, he gave to the priests a copy of the Torah (Deuteronomy 31:26). Then he taught the people a song of praise, which began with these words:

> Give ear, O heavens, and I will speak;
>> And hear, O earth, the words of my mouth.
> Let my teaching drop as the rain,
>> My speech distill as the dew,
> As raindrops on the tender herb,
>> And as showers on the grass.
> For I proclaim the name of the LORD:
>> Ascribe greatness to our God.
> He is the Rock, His work is perfect;
>> For all His ways are justice,
> A God of truth and without injustice;
>> Righteous and upright is He (Deuteronomy 32:1-4).

After his song was finished, Moses blessed the people, ascended to the top of Mount Pisgah, and died in the presence of the LORD (Deuteronomy 34:1-5).

Other great moments in the Old Testament were celebrated in worship, especially with the singing of songs. Deborah and Barak rejoiced in song when God delivered them from the Canaanite armies of Sisera (Judges 5). Hannah celebrated the birth of her son Samuel, who was born in answer to her fervent prayers (1 Samuel

2). David spoke his last words in the form of a beautiful song just before his death (2 Samuel 23:1-7). The disobedient prophet Jonah, after he had been delivered from the belly of the fish, worshiped God for his salvation (Jonah 2).

A great multitude of texts throughout the Old Testament attest to the importance of worship. Over and over, the Bible invites and commands God's people to sing, to worship, to serve, to pray, to rejoice, to call out to God, to dance, to play instruments, to bring offerings, to enter the temple, and so on. For example, the prophet Jeremiah encourages us:

> Sing to the LORD!
> Praise the LORD!" (Jeremiah 20:13).

Joel prophesied,

> You shall eat in plenty and be satisfied,
> And praise the name of the LORD your God (Joel 2:26).

In the Old Testament, worship may involve the individual, the family, or the congregation. Cain and Abel offered sacrifices as individuals (Genesis 4:3-4). After the flood, Noah built an altar and worshiped with his family (Genesis 8:20-22), and God was pleased with the sacrifice. Throughout his journeys, Abraham built altars where he would lead his family in worship (Genesis 12:7, 8; 13:4, 18). We read that Isaac "built an altar and called upon the name of the LORD" (Genesis 26:25); and more than once, Jacob built altars, whether for individual worship or for family worship (Genesis 33:20; 35:7). Moses built an altar in the wilderness, and the tabernacle had a permanent altar for the people of Israel (Exodus 17:15; 20:24-26). As soon as Joshua brought Israel into the Promised Land, he built an altar and led the people in worship (Joshua 8:30). Job offered sacrifices regularly on behalf of his children (Job 1:5). The first Psalm opens with a reference to the individual ("Blessed is the man", Psalm 1:1), but it concludes with statements about the "congregation" (Psalm 1:5) and "the righteous ones" (Psalm 1:6), which emphasize the participation of the entire Church. Throughout the psalms, we find both individual prayers and communal prayers, individual testimonies and communal testimonies, individual praises and communal praises. Therefore, biblical worship is both private and congregational. Even when worshiping alone, the worshiper is part of the people of God. In anticipation of gathering together with God's people for worship, the psalmist writes, "I will give you thanks in the great assembly; I will praise you among many people" (Psalm 35:18). And looking back on previous times of worship, the author of Psalm 40 declares, "I have not concealed your steadfast love and your truth from the great assembly" (Psalm 40:11). In the Old Testament, worship may be an individual affair, or it may be the shared activity of a family or of the entire people of God.

6. The New Testament stresses the importance of worship

The New Testament accepts all of the Old Testament background regarding worship, and then it adds further amplifications. In the New Testament Church, our worship also includes reflection on the death and resurrection of Christ. Our worship includes the sacraments, such as water baptism, the LORD's Supper, and foot washing. Through our worship, we devote ourselves to "the apostles' teaching and the fellowship, to the breaking of bread and the prayers" (Acts 2:42). After the incarnation of Jesus, worship became even more important than ever before. In fact, when Jesus approached Jerusalem on the Sunday before Passover (what we call the Triumphal Entry), his followers began to rejoice and praise God. They declared Jesus as their King, and the Pharisees grew angry and told Jesus to rebuke his disciples. Jesus, however, made this astonishing claim: "I tell you that if these should keep silent, the stones would immediately cry out" (Luke 19:37-40).

The New Testament Church should be a vibrant center of healing and transformation that engages culture and reaches out to the community. Worship is a part of that process of healing and transformation. Our worship includes the prayers of the saints and the songs of Zion. Our worship is one way that we pass on the faith to our children and grandchildren.

When I think of worship, I think of the New Testament character Anna. She was a widow, eighty-four years old: "She did not depart from the temple, worshiping with fasting and prayer night and day" (Luke 2:37). When I think of worship, I think of Mary the mother of Jesus, who offers to God a song of worship and praise. When Mary hears the prophetic blessing of Elizabeth, she responds with an outburst of worship, saying,

My soul magnifies the LORD,
And my spirit has rejoiced in God my Savior.
For He has regarded the lowly state of His maidservant;
For behold, henceforth all generations will call me blessed.
For He who is mighty has done great things for me,
And holy is His name.
And His mercy is on those who fear Him
From generation to generation (Luke 1:46-50 NKJ).

When I think of worship, I think of Jesus Christ, of whom the Scripture says, "as His custom was, He went into the synagogue on the Sabbath day" (Luke 4:16). When I think of worship, I think of these words in the book of Hebrews: "Therefore by Him let us continually offer the sacrifice of praise to God, that is, the fruit of our lips, giving thanks to His name" (Hebrews 13:15).

I think of Paul's word to the Ephesian church: "be filled with the Spirit, speaking to one another in psalms and hymns and spiritual songs, singing and making melody in your heart to the LORD" (Ephesians 5:18-19). I think of his exhortations to the Romans: "Praise the LORD, all you Gentiles! Laud Him, all you peoples!" (Romans 15:11). More than anything, however, when I think about worship, I think about the message of Jesus to the Samaritan woman: "the hour is coming, and now is, when the true worshipers will worship the Father in spirit and truth; for the Father is seeking such to worship Him. God is Spirit, and those who worship Him must worship in spirit and truth" (John 4:23-24).

Worship was so important to the early Church that they worshiped in the temple daily. We read the following in the book of Acts:

So, continuing daily with one accord in the temple, and breaking bread from house to house, they ate their food with gladness and simplicity of heart, praising God and having favor with all the people. And the LORD added to the church daily those who were being saved (Acts 2:46-47).

For the early Church, daily worship and continual praise were a way of life. Because of their dedication, the LORD added new converts to the Body of Christ.

D. Worship is our ultimate destiny

Humanity was created to live in a loving relationship with God, and humanity is destined to live forever with him where they will worship and praise God while enjoying the glory of his presence. In the book of Revelation, John is taken up into heaven, and he sees a vision of God, who sits enthroned in glory and beauty surrounded by the four living creatures and the twenty-four elders. The four living creatures are worshiping God without ceasing as they cry out day and night,

> Holy, holy, holy,
> LORD God Almighty,
> Who was and is and is to come! (Revelation 4:8).

Likewise, the twenty-four elders fall down before God and worship him as they exclaim,

> You are worthy, O LORD,
>   To receive glory and honor and power;
> For You created all things,
>   And by Your will they
>   exist and were created (Revelation 4:11).

John then sees in the hand of God a scroll, and the Lamb of God comes and takes the scroll out of the right hand of Him who sat upon the throne. When he takes the scroll, the four living creatures and the twenty-four elders fall down before the Lamb and begin to sing a new song of worship:

> You are worthy to take the scroll,
> And to open its seals;
> For You were slain,
> And have redeemed us to God by Your blood
> Out of every tribe and tongue and people and nation,
> And have made us kings and priests to our God;
> And we shall reign on the earth" (Revelation 5:9-10).

At that point, John realizes the full extent of the heavenly worship, and he relates his vision in these words:

> Then I looked, and I heard the voice of many angels around the throne, the living creatures, and the elders; and the number of them was ten thousand times ten thousand, and thousands of thousands, saying with a loud voice:
>
> > Worthy is the Lamb who was slain
> > To receive power and riches and wisdom,
> > And strength and honor and glory and blessing!
>
> And every creature which is in heaven and on the earth and under the earth and such as are in the sea, and all that are in them, I heard saying:
>
> > Blessing and honor and glory and power
> > Be to Him who sits on the throne,
> > And to the Lamb, forever and ever!
>
> Then the four living creatures said, "Amen!" And the twenty-four elders fell down and worshiped Him who lives forever and ever (Revelation 5:11-14).

Later in John's visions of heaven, he tells about the great multitude of God's people who stand before the throne of God and worship him day and night. John describes the vast congregation of worshipers with these words:

> After these things I looked, and behold, a great multitude which no one could number, of all nations, tribes, peoples, and tongues, standing before the throne and before the Lamb, clothed with white robes, with palm branches in their hands … Therefore they are before the throne of God, and serve Him day and night in His temple. And He who sits on the throne will dwell among them (Revelation 7:9-15).

True worship is so important, that God pours out his wrath upon all those who engage in false worship (Revelation 9:20). An angel flies across the land, proclaiming the everlasting gospel, and encouraging everyone to worship God. The angel says, "Fear God and give glory to Him, for the hour of His judgment has come; and worship Him who made heaven and earth, the sea and springs of water" (Revelation 14:7). Another angel then warns that whoever worships the beast will be cast into the lake of fire (Revelation 14:9-11; 16:2; 19:20).

Once again, John sees a vision of the redeemed as they stand on the sea of glass, having harps of God:

> They sing the song of Moses, the servant of God, and the song of the Lamb, saying:
>
> > Great and marvelous *are* Your works
> > > LORD God Almighty!
> > Just and true *are* Your ways,
> > > O King of the saints!
> > Who shall not fear You, O LORD, and glorify Your name?
> > > For *You* alone *are* holy.
> > For all nations shall come and worship before You,
> > > For Your judgments have been manifested
> > > > (Revelation 15:3-4).

This demonstrates that the goal of history is for all the nations to come and worship God. The psalmist had stated the same fact many hundreds of years earlier. We read these powerful prophecies in the book of Psalms:

> All the ends of the world
> > Shall remember and turn to the LORD,
> And all the families of the nations
> > Shall worship before You.
> For the kingdom is the LORD's,
> > And He rules over the nations (Psalm 22:27-28).

> All the earth shall worship You
> > And sing praises to You;
> They shall sing praises to Your name (Psalm 66:4).

> All nations whom You have made
> > Shall come and worship before You, O LORD,
> And shall glorify Your name.
> > For You are great, and do wondrous things;
> You alone are God (Psalm 86:9-10).

Conclusion

In summary, worship is important because we were created to worship God, and our eternal destiny will be to worship God. Taken together, these two points make worship our highest occupation. Our salvation and our love for God demand that we worship him out of gratitude and devotion. Furthermore, our relationship to God is sustained by worship – without worship, our relationship to God would wither and die. Worship is life-giving breath to our spirits. The importance of worship is shown by the fact that the Heavenly Father takes pleasure in our worship, and he seeks after people who will worship him.

Questions for Review and Application

1. Explain why the topic of worship is important in the world today.

2. Describe the different styles of worship in contemporary churches.

3. How do worship and idolatry relate to the everyday life of the Christian?

4. Write down one Bible verse that shows the relationship between worship and spirituality.

5. Explain how the Pentecostal movement has impacted the practice of worship throughout the world.

6. What is the difference between the faith of a Christian and the faith of demons?

7. What are some things that God does when he finds our worship pleasing to him?

8. Tell how worship is a fulfillment of the great commandment to love God with all of our hearts.

9. Describe the two ways that worship enhances our worth.

10. List four Scripture references in which God commands us to worship.

11. Did worship originate with Adam and Eve? If not, when did worship originate?

12. Explain the purpose of God's creation.

13. List the four crucial questions regarding our reason for existence.

14. Describe how the first and second Commandments encourage us to worship God.

15. Why did the Israelites sing a song after their deliverance from Egyptian bondage?

16. Name four occasions in the Old Testament that were celebrated by means of worship.

17. In what ways does the New Testament amplify the Old Testament's teaching on worship?

18. Write out what you consider to be the most powerful Bible verse regarding worship as our ultimate destiny.

# CHAPTER 2

THE DEFINITION OF TRUE WORSHIP

Fear God and give glory to Him ... worship Him who made heaven and earth (Revelation 14:7).

Chapter 1 served as an introduction to our study by showing the importance of worship. This chapter will help us discover the nature and definition of true worship. The Church gathers every week for worship, so we are inclined to believe that we know everything that we need to know about worship. However, the goal of this book is to make us examine our worship practices and to cause us to seek for God's direction in our worship.

A. What is worship?

Before going any further, it may be helpful to sharpen our study by defining the word 'worship'. Some people think that worship only consists of singing, as in the phrase 'praise and worship'. While it is true that singing can be an expression of worship, worship is much more than just singing. Some people think of worship as a Sunday morning event where people gather to worship. It is true that we can call the Sunday services 'worship', but again, worship involves more than what we do in our church services.

One dictionary states that to worship is "To honour or revere as a supernatural being or power, or as a holy thing; to regard or approach with veneration; to adore with appropriate acts, rites, or ceremonies."[1] Similarly, another dictionary defines worship as "reverence offered a divine being or supernatural power; also: an act of

---

[1] *Oxford English Dictionary Online* (Oxford University Press, 2016).

expressing such reverence."[2] Old Testament scholar Daniel Block defines worship this way: "True worship involves reverential human acts of submission and homage before the divine Sovereign in response to his gracious revelation of himself and in accord with his will."[3] Alfred P. Gibbs offers a definition that emphasizes the spiritual attitude of the worshiper. He writes, "Worship is the occupation of the heart, not with its needs, or even with its blessings, but with God Himself."[4] Clearly, Gibbs' definition emphasizes two important characteristics of true worship: 1. Worship must come from the heart. 2. Worship must be focused upon God, not upon ourselves. While each of these definitions is helpful, our source of ultimate authority is the Scripture. Therefore, at this point we will examine the biblical terminology used to define true worship.

B. Old Testament terminology regarding worship

The Old Testament uses three primary terms that are translated 'worship'. The first term is *avad* (usually translated 'to serve'), which signifies a lifestyle of commitment and allegiance. The second term is *yireh* (usually translated 'to fear'), which refers to the attitude of fear and reverence. The third term is *havah* (usually translated 'to worship'), which fundamentally means the act of bowing down to pay homage. Although these Hebrew words are most often translated as 'to serve', 'to fear', and 'to worship', they each refer to certain aspects of worship. We will examine each of them in more detail.

1. Serve: A lifestyle of worship
The Old Testament speaks of worship as 'serving' God. When the LORD calls Israel to meet with him on Mount Sinai, he says to them, "you shall **serve** God on this mountain" (Exodus 3:12). To serve God means to devote oneself fully to God. Serving God is a commitment to total allegiance, a lifestyle of dedication to God

---

[2] *Merriam-Webster's Collegiate Dictionary* (Springfield, MA: Merriam-Webster, 11th edn, 2003).

[3] Daniel I. Block, *For the Glory of God: Recovering a Biblical Theology of Worship* (Grand Rapids, MI: Baker Academic, 2014), p. 29.

[4] Alfred P. Gibbs, *Worship: The Christian's Highest Occupation* (Kansas City, KS: Walterick Publishers, 2nd edn, 1960), p. 16.

and to God alone. To serve God means to give honor and glory to God through a daily lifestyle of obedience and behavior that reflects a committed relationship. Although worship can be expressed through specific actions like praising God, giving to God, and singing to God, worship is also a lifestyle of devotion and holiness that honors God. The Old Testament includes more than fifty references to worship as serving God. These references demonstrate the following important characteristics of worship.

a. Serving the LORD is a choice

After the Israelites enter the Promised Land, Joshua calls them together so that they might rededicate themselves to the LORD. Joshua challenges them to make a decision. He says, "And if it seems evil to you to **serve** the LORD, choose for yourselves this day whom you will **serve**, whether the gods which your fathers **served** that were on the other side of the River, or the gods of the Amorites, in whose land you dwell. But as for me and my house, we will **serve** the LORD" (Joshua 24:15). God offers his grace to us, and he allows us the freedom to choose whether or not we will worship him with all of our hearts.

b. Serving the LORD is absolute

If we make a commitment to serve the LORD, we cannot serve any other gods. When the LORD gave Israel the Ten Commandments, he warned them not to worship idols. He said, "you shall not bow down to them nor **serve** them" (Exodus 20:5). God also warned them that they should not "serve" the gods of the Canaanites (Exodus 23:23-24). Israel's major problem throughout the Old Testament was their tendency to worship other gods. Consider the following example:

> So the people served the LORD all the days of Joshua … When all that generation had been gathered to their fathers, another generation arose after them who did not know the LORD nor the work which He had done for Israel. Then the children of Israel did evil in the sight of the LORD, and **served** the Baals (Judges 2:7-13).

Eventually, the LORD punished the Israelites because "they **served** idols" continually (2 Kings 17:12). God is merciful, but if we continue to serve other gods, we will be punished.

c. Serving the LORD requires surrender

King Hezekiah reminds the Israelites of the necessity of repentance and total surrender when they enter the temple of God to worship: "Now do not be stiff-necked, as your fathers were, but yield yourselves to the LORD; and enter His sanctuary, which He has sanctified forever, and **serve** the LORD your God, that the fierceness of His wrath may turn away from you" (2 Chronicles 30:8). Hezekiah was a righteous king, and he restored true worship in Israel.

d. Serving the LORD should be enthusiastic

Before Moses died, he explained to the Israelites the nature of their relationship to God. Moses declared, "And now, Israel, what does the LORD your God require of you, but ... **serve** the LORD your God with all your heart and with all your soul" (Deuteronomy 10:12). Worship is not acceptable to God if it does not come from the heart. We are commanded to love God with all of our hearts; and, in the same fashion, we are commanded to worship God with all of our hearts.

e. Serving the LORD requires steadfastness

In the days of the prophet Samuel, the Israelites had backslidden and failed God. Samuel gathered them together to encourage repentance and restoration. "Then Samuel said to the people, 'Do not fear. You have done all this wickedness; yet do not turn aside from following the LORD, but **serve** the LORD with all your heart'" (1 Samuel 12:20). After making the decision to serve God, we must be determined, unwavering, and resolute.

f. Serving the LORD should be joyful

Worship is a lifestyle of serving God, but our service is with thankfulness and with joy. We are serving the God who has saved us from the bondage of sin. Some people think of worship as an obligation, a duty, and a burden. Although I would agree that we are obligated to worship, the Bible speaks of worship as a time of celebration and rejoicing, not as a burden. The psalmist writes,

Make a joyful shout to the LORD, all you lands!
   Serve the LORD with gladness;
   Come before His presence with singing" (Psalm 100:1-2).

g. Serving the LORD is a qualification for eternal blessing
The prophet Malachi speaks of the day of judgment, when the people who serve the LORD will be counted as God's "jewels." On that day, declares the prophet,

Then you shall again discern
   Between the righteous and the wicked,
Between one who **serves** God
   And one who does not **serve** Him" (Malachi 3:18).

In summary, when the Old Testament uses the word 'to serve' to describe a lifestyle of devotion to God, it indicates that worship is expressed first and foremost through total allegiance to God. Everything that we do – our work, our play, our church, our witness, our joys, our sufferings – should be considered an offering of worship to the glory and honor of God.

2. Fear: An attitude of worship

The word 'fear' is another term that can mean 'worship'. References to fearing God or fearing the LORD occur more than eighty times in the Old Testament. Although it can mean "to be terrified or scared," fear can also mean "to reverence and honor." It is this idea of honor and reverence that makes the fear of the LORD suitable as an attitude of worship.

a. Fearing the LORD and serving the LORD go together
After the Israelites had dedicated themselves to serve the LORD, Joshua added the following instructions: "Now therefore, **fear** the LORD, serve Him in sincerity and in truth" (Joshua 24:14). The promise to serve God cannot be fulfilled unless the fear of the LORD is present. To fear God is to have reverence and awe for his power and authority as God.

b. Fearing God is a response to grace
The psalmist insists that when we experience the power of God's forgiveness, we will respond with reverence toward him.

But there is forgiveness with You,
That You may be feared. (Psalm 130:4).

The fear of God is an inner disposition or attitude of deep respect for God. Therefore, it represents the emotional foundation of worship. True worship holds God in high esteem. True worship never takes God for granted but respects God's ultimate authority.

c. Fearing anything except the LORD is equal to idolatry
In the days of Gideon, the LORD sends a prophet to warn the Israelites concerning their worship of other gods. The LORD says, "I am the LORD your God; do not **fear** the gods of the Amorites, in whose land you dwell. But you have not obeyed My voice" (Judges 6:10). When the Israelites had entered the Promised Land, they had been commanded to tear down the altars of the people in the land, but they had failed to do so. Instead, they began to worship the gods of the land.

Other biblical passages show that fearing other gods is equal to worshiping them, For example:

then beware, lest you forget the LORD who brought you out of the land of Egypt, from the house of bondage. You shall **fear** the LORD your God and serve Him, and shall take oaths in His name. You shall not go after other gods, the gods of the peoples who are all around you (Deuteronomy 6:12-14).

When speaking of lifeless idols, Jeremiah declares,

Do not be **afraid** of them,
For they cannot do evil,
Nor can they do any good" (Jeremiah 10:5).

Jeremiah is saying that since idols are powerless, they are undeserving of fear. However, Jeremiah insists that it is the LORD who should be feared:

Who would not **fear** You,
O King of the nations?

For this is Your rightful due (Jeremiah 10:7).

The verb 'to fear' is used in these biblical texts with the meaning 'to worship', 'to reverence' and 'to serve'.[5] The word 'fear', therefore, is substituted for other words denoting worship and service. Although the LORD demands exclusive worship, the Israelites (and today's Christians) are tempted to worship many gods. The people in 2 Kings 17, for example, "feared the LORD" but continued to also worship other gods (2 Kings 17:33). The worship of many gods was normal in ancient times – the Assyrians, the Babylonians, the Canaanites, the Egyptians, the Greeks, the Persians, and the Romans worshiped many gods. However, Israel was called to be different. Israel made a commitment to worship the LORD alone.

d. The fear of the LORD is different from other kinds of fear
Power attracts and provokes wonder, but it does not necessarily give rise to trust and love; and it is on this count that the fear of the LORD is different from the fear of other powers. The LORD asks that the Israelites worship him not only because of his might, but also because of his mercy. The LORD defeated the gods of Egypt and showed himself superior in strength, but his acts go beyond a simple demonstration of power. The LORD's power is exercised toward the purpose of salvation in bringing the Israelites out of slavery, and the covenant is founded upon this expression of divine care. Moses declares to the Israelites that they are chosen by the LORD, not because of their own attributes

> but because the LORD loves you, and because He would keep the oath which He swore to your fathers, the LORD has brought you out with a mighty hand, and redeemed you from the house of bondage, from the hand of Pharaoh king of Egypt (Deuteronomy 7:8).

Furthermore, Moses draws attention to the LORD's affection, his love for Israel:

> Indeed heaven and the highest heavens belong to the LORD your God, also the earth with all that is in it. The LORD delighted only in your fathers, to **love** them; and He chose their

---

[5] David J.A. Clines, *Dictionary of Classical Hebrew* (8 vols.; Sheffield: Sheffield Academic Press, 1993), IV, p. 278.

descendants after them, you above all peoples, as it is this day (Deuteronomy 10:14-15).

Therefore, because salvation is based upon God's love, he asks that we express a depth of worship that exceeds fear and reverence. God's love calls forth the kind of worship that is based upon our affection, devotion, and love for God. Moses commands the Israelites, "And now, Israel, what does the LORD your God require of you, but to **fear** the LORD your God, to walk in all His ways and to **love** Him" (Deuteronomy 10:12). Moses adds further,

> You shall **fear** the LORD your God ... He is your praise, and He is your God, who has done for you these great and awesome things which your eyes have seen ... Therefore you shall **love** the LORD your God (Deuteronomy 10:20-11:1).

Thus, when the LORD tells Israel not to fear other gods, he is insisting that his saving grace makes him the only God worthy of worship. His love for the Israelites calls for their reciprocation in worship, and his gracious acts of salvation require the Israelites' exclusive reverence and fear.

To summarize, the word 'serve' speaks of worship as a lifestyle, and the word 'fear' speaks of worship as an inner attitude. True worship includes the inner disposition of respect, honor, and reverence for God. It remains for us to examine the third Old Testament word for worship.

3. Bowing down: Actions of worship

The third Old Testament term that we will consider is *havah* (usually translated 'to worship'), which fundamentally means the act of bowing down to pay homage. In Old Testament times, the root meaning (bowing or kneeling down) is expanded to include any act of worship or any ritual action that pays homage to God and that expresses veneration to God. These actions include feasts, sacrifices, prayers, songs, art, music, or dance. They can be formal liturgical acts, ceremonies in private, worship acts within the family, or any expression of worship in the Church. These acts of worship include essentially any intentional expression of praise or thanksgiving.

a. Worship is connected to the fear of the LORD

The following text from 2 Kings shows how the worship of the LORD can be described by the use of several different terms, even within one verse:

> but the LORD, who brought you up from the land of Egypt with great power and an outstretched arm, Him you shall fear, Him you shall **worship**, and to Him you shall offer sacrifice (2 Kings 17:36. See also Psalm 5:7).

b. Worship involves the giving of ourselves to God

The word 'worship' (*havah*) is used for the first time in the story of Abraham's sacrifice of Isaac. The LORD tests Abraham and commands him to sacrifice Isaac his only son. When Abraham's party reaches the mountain where the sacrifice is to take place, we read the following:

> And Abraham said to his young men, "Stay here with the donkey; the lad and I will go yonder and **worship**, and we will come back to you" (Genesis 22:5).

Whether it be the giving of Abraham's son, the giving of a lamb, the giving of money, or the giving of our time, worship involves giving to God something that is valuable to us.

c. Worship is a proper response to answered prayer

When Abraham was old, his son Isaac had not yet married; therefore, Abraham's servant was sent to find a wife for Isaac. The servant prayed earnestly that the LORD would direct him to the right family and to the right woman who would marry Isaac. As soon as the LORD answered the servant's prayer and he was assured that he had found the right woman, "Then the man bowed down his head and **worshiped** the LORD" (Genesis 24:26).

Another example of answered prayer is found in the book of Exodus. The people cried out to the LORD for deliverance from their Egyptian oppressors, and God sent Moses to bring them out of Egypt. When Moses revealed himself to the people, they worshiped the LORD: "So the people believed; and when they heard that the LORD had visited the children of Israel and that He had looked on their affliction, then they bowed their heads and **worshiped**" (Exodus 4:31). It is important to notice that the people worshiped the LORD as soon as they received God's promise of salvation. They did not wait until the salvation had been accomplished! On the night before they were to leave Egypt, Moses explained the significance of the Passover meal, and they once again worshiped the LORD: "you shall say, 'It is the Passover sacrifice of the LORD, who passed over the houses of the children of Israel in Egypt when He struck the Egyptians and delivered our households.' So the people bowed their heads and **worshiped**" (Exodus 12:27).

Many other examples of worship in answer to prayer might be cited. The story of Gideon is a powerful incentive for us to trust God. Over and over, the LORD promised Gideon that he would win the battle against the Midianites, but Gideon was not convinced. Finally, Gideon and his servant sneaked into the enemy camp to spy on them. Gideon overheard a Midianite soldier recounting a dream in which the Midianite camp was destroyed. The story continues:

> Then his companion answered and said, "This is nothing else but the sword of Gideon the son of Joash, a man of Israel! Into his hand God has delivered Midian and the whole camp." And so it was, when Gideon heard the telling of the dream and its interpretation, that he **worshiped**. He returned to the camp of Israel, and said, "Arise, for the LORD has delivered the camp of Midian into your hand" (Judges 7:14-15).

d. Worship of other gods is forbidden

After they are saved from Egyptian bondage, the Israelites make a covenant with the LORD to worship him only (Exodus 20:1-5). However, as they journey through the wilderness, they give in to the temptation of idolatry. When the LORD sees the golden calf that they had made, he says,

> They have turned aside quickly out of the way which I commanded them. They have made themselves a molded calf, and **worshiped** it and sacrificed to it, and said, "This *is* your god, O Israel, that brought you out of the land of Egypt!" (Exodus 32:8).

He then repeats his commandment forbidding idolatry of any kind. The LORD says, "for you shall **worship** no other god, for the LORD, whose name is Jealous, is a jealous God" (Exodus 34:13-14). The LORD's hatred of idolatry is so great, that he threatens his people with severe punishment if they are found worshiping idols: "Then it shall be, if you by any means forget the LORD your God, and follow other gods, and serve them and **worship** them, I testify against you this day that you shall surely perish" (Deuteronomy 8:19).

e. Worship is the normal response to God's presence
I have heard ministers say that we should worship God when we feel like it, and we should worship even if we do not feel like it. That is a true statement, but when the presence of God is manifested in the Church, worship seems to be the only appropriate response. After Israel's tabernacle in the wilderness was completed, the people gathered together to witness what would happen.

> And it came to pass, when Moses entered the tabernacle, that the pillar of cloud descended and stood at the door of the tabernacle, and the LORD talked with Moses. All the people saw the pillar of cloud standing at the tabernacle door, and all the people rose and **worshiped**, each man in his tent door (Exodus 33:9-10).

The people saw the presence of God, and they were moved to worship. Very soon afterwards, Moses himself was allowed to stand in the cleft of the rock and to see the glory of the LORD. His vision of God caused him to worship:

> Now the LORD descended in the cloud and stood with him there, and proclaimed the name of the LORD. And the LORD passed before him and proclaimed, "The LORD, the LORD God, merciful and gracious, longsuffering, and abounding in goodness and truth, keeping mercy for thousands, forgiving iniquity and transgression and sin, by no means clearing the guilty, visiting the iniquity of the fathers upon the children and the children's children to the third and the fourth generation." So Moses made haste and bowed his head toward the earth, and **worshiped** (Exodus 34:5-8).

f. Some activities are unacceptable in worship

When the Israelites reached the Promised Land, they encountered the Canaanites, who practiced a variety of unacceptable methods of worship. Therefore, the LORD said,

> You shall not **worship** the LORD your God in that way; for every abomination to the LORD which He hates they have done to their gods; for they burn even their sons and daughters in the fire to their gods (Deuteronomy 12:31).

Besides burning their children in the fire, the Canaanites engaged in other occult practices, which the LORD hated. This is what the LORD said concerning those forbidden worship practices:

> When you come into the land which the LORD your God is giving you, you shall not learn to follow the abominations of those nations. There shall not be found among you anyone who makes his son or his daughter pass through the fire, or one who practices witchcraft, or a soothsayer, or one who interprets omens, or a sorcerer, or one who conjures spells, or a medium, or a spiritist, or one who calls up the dead. For all who do these things are an abomination to the LORD, and because of these abominations the LORD your God drives them out from before you (Deuteronomy 18:9-12).

g. Worship includes giving our best to God

The Hebrew word *havah* is more than a worshipful attitude – it involves specific acts of giving to God. For example, the Israelites were told that they should bring their firstfruits (tithe) to the LORD. This act of giving was a vital part of worship:

> Then you shall set it (the firstfruits) before the LORD your God, and **worship** before the LORD your God. So you shall rejoice in every good thing which the LORD your God has given to you and your house, you and the Levite and the stranger who is among you. (Deuteronomy 26:10-11).

Giving to God should be an act of worship, and it should be a joyful act. We should "rejoice in every good thing which the LORD" our God has given to us.

h. Worship is the appropriate response to tragedy

David's terrible sin against Bathsheba and her husband Uriah resulted in God's judgment of David. The penalty for David's sin was the death of the infant child who had been conceived in the adulterous relationship. David fasted for seven days and prayed that the child might be healed. Unfortunately, the judgment of God was severe, and the child died. We read what happened next:

> When David saw that his servants were whispering, David perceived that the child was dead. Therefore David said to his servants, "Is the child dead?" And they said, "He is dead." So David arose from the ground, washed and anointed himself, and changed his clothes; and he went into the house of the LORD and **worshiped** (2 Samuel 12:19-20).

David hoped and prayed that the child might live, but he was terribly disappointed. His child died, and David grieved. However, in his most desperate hour, at his lowest point, he did not withdraw from God's presence. On the contrary, he drew near to God and worshiped. Worship is the best response to the challenges and setbacks of life.

We learn a similar lesson from another tragic episode – the story of Job. The Bible tells us that Job was a prosperous man with a wife and seven children. Faithful in his service to the LORD, he offered sacrifices regularly on behalf of his children. However, when God gives Satan permission to attack him, Job suffers a series of losses. First, the Sabeans came and stole his oxen and donkeys, killing his servants. Second, fire came down from heaven and killed his sheep and the servants keeping them. Third, the Chaldeans took his camels and killed the servants who attended the camels. Finally, a great wind blew in from the desert, destroying the house of his eldest son and killing all seven of Job's children. Surely, Job must have gone into shock and deep grief. He could have cried out and accused God of causing these tragedies. He could have committed suicide; but, instead, Job did the following:

> Then Job arose, tore his robe, and shaved his head; and he fell to the ground and **worshiped**. And he said: "Naked I came from

my mother's womb, And naked shall I return there. The LORD gave, and the LORD has taken away; Blessed be the name of the LORD (Job 1:14-21).

In his darkest hour, Job worshiped God. Worship is the proper action for us to take when faced with tragedy.

i. Worship is the act of exalting and honoring God for his attributes

One of the greatest descriptions of worship was written by King David to celebrate the installation of the Ark of the Covenant in the Tabernacle in Jerusalem. The ark had been taken out of the Tabernacle many years earlier during a battle with the Philistines. Although the Ark was soon restored to Israel, it remained outside of Jerusalem until David brought it back. To commemorate the occasion, David wrote a psalm, which says in part,

> Sing to the LORD, all the earth;
>   Proclaim the good news of His salvation from day to day.
> Declare His glory among the nations,
>   His wonders among all peoples.
> For the LORD is great and greatly to be praised;
>   He is also to be feared above all gods.
> For all the gods of the peoples are idols,
>   But the LORD made the heavens.
> Honor and majesty are before Him;
>   Strength and gladness are in His place.
> Give to the LORD, O families of the peoples,
>   Give to the LORD glory and strength.
> Give to the LORD the glory due His name;
>   Bring an offering, and come before Him.
> Oh, **worship** the LORD in the beauty of holiness!
>   Tremble before Him, all the earth.
> The world also is firmly established,
>   It shall not be moved.
> Let the heavens rejoice, and let the earth be glad;
>   And let them say among the nations, "The LORD reigns" (1 Chronicles 16:23-31).

David encourages the people to worship the LORD in the beauty of holiness (See also Psalm 29:2). This worship includes specific actions, such as singing, praising, offering, trembling, rejoicing, and proclaiming God's majestic attributes. Worship involves actions. Although worship should be a lifestyle and an attitude of reverence, it must be more.

j. Worship produces victory

While worship is naturally and easily offered after we have won a great victory, it also is an important ingredient to the preparations for battle. Worship flows freely after prayer has been answered, but it also should be offered before the answer comes. Worship prepares us for victory by building our faith and by creating an atmosphere of anticipation and expectation. When Israel was facing the threat of an army that vastly outnumbered them, the LORD spoke to them through a prophet and gave instructions for victory. The prophet said,

> Listen, all you of Judah and you inhabitants of Jerusalem, and you, King Jehoshaphat! Thus says the LORD to you: 'Do not be afraid nor dismayed because of this great multitude, for the battle is not yours, but God's ... You will not need to fight in this battle. Position yourselves, stand still and see the salvation of the LORD, who is with you, O Judah and Jerusalem!' Do not fear or be dismayed; tomorrow go out against them, for the LORD is with you. And Jehoshaphat bowed his head with his face to the ground, and all Judah and the inhabitants of Jerusalem bowed before the LORD, **worshiping** the LORD (2 Chronicles 20:15-18).

The enemy was formidable, and the battle had not even begun, but Jehoshaphat and the people worshiped the LORD. God gave the promise of victory, and the Israelites believed God's promise; therefore, they worshiped in faith and expectation. Whenever we face the enemy, we should worship God before entering the battle. The Israelites went up to fight, singing and praising as they went, and the LORD gave them victory that day.

k. Worship is a companion to the reading of Scripture

As we learned above, God speaks through the prophets; and, when he speaks, the people should worship God. However, God also speaks through Scripture. Unfortunately, many Christians do not understand the deep connection between Scripture and worship. They view worship and preaching as two different things. They separate worship from the teaching of Scripture as well. These perspectives are not biblical. In the Bible, worship, preaching, and teaching are closely connected. The book of Nehemiah relates the events surrounding Ezra's reading of Scripture to the Israelites:

> And Ezra opened the book in the sight of all the people, for he was standing above all the people; and when he opened it, all the people stood up. And Ezra blessed the LORD, the great God. Then all the people answered, "Amen, Amen!" while lifting up their hands. And they bowed their heads and **worshiped** the LORD with their faces to the ground (Nehemiah 8:5-6).

We very often take the Bible for granted. We are tempted to treat it lightly. However, we learn from this text in Nehemiah that the reading of Scripture is a great occasion for worship! We believe that Scripture is the inspired Word of God, so let us worship. We believe that God's Word will not pass away, so let us worship. We believe that the Bible is God's message to us, so let us worship him!

C. New Testament terminology regarding worship

The New Testament terms for 'worship' are quite similar to those found in the Old Testament. They can be organized according to the same headings as we used in the previous section: 'to serve', 'to fear', and 'to bow down'.

1. Serve: A lifestyle of worship

The New Testament writers use two specific terms that relate to worship as a lifestyle of service that honors and glorifies God. The first is the Greek word *latreia* (and its verbal form, *latreuo*), which means "service in worship to God." The second is the Greek term *sebomai*, which signifies a person who is a worshiper of God. The significance of these terms can be seen in the following Scripture passages.

a. Worship is the giving of ourselves as a living sacrifice

The most important New Testament text regarding worship as a lifestyle is probably Paul's admonition to the Romans. He writes, "I beseech you therefore, brethren, by the mercies of God, that you present your bodies a living sacrifice, holy, acceptable to God, which is your reasonable **service**" (Romans 12:1). The apostle Paul declares that our worship to God must include our whole selves, which includes our bodies. In the Old Testament, the people offered sacrifices of bulls, goats, sheep, and birds; but after the death of Christ, those animal sacrifices were no longer valid. Their ultimate purpose was to point to Jesus Christ, and his death on the cross was the fulfillment of the sacrificial system. However, Paul indicates that Christians must offer up their lives to Christ. In other words, we no longer worship God by means of occasional sacrifices of animals. Instead, we worship God continually through the daily sacrifice of our bodies to a lifestyle of service. We offer ourselves as "living sacrifices" to God. This is why Paul could insist, "whatever you do, do all to the glory of God" (1 Corinthians 10:31). He also said that whatever we do, we should do it "as bondservants of Christ, doing the will of God from the heart" (Ephesians 6:6).

b. Worship is the continual practice of believers

To offer ourselves as a living sacrifice means that we serve God continually. Paul's hope in the promise of God caused him to serve God night and day. He writes: "To this promise our twelve tribes, earnestly **serving** God night and day, hope to attain. For this hope's sake, King Agrippa, I am accused by the Jews" (Acts 26:7). With hope in that same promise, the widow Anna looked for the coming of the Messiah. She is described in the following way: "and this woman was a widow of about eighty-four years, who did not depart from the temple, but **served** God with fastings and prayers night and day" (Luke 2:37). Not only should our worship continue night and day, but this lifestyle of worship must continue until we meet the LORD. Zacharias, the father of John the Baptist spoke this prayer:

To grant us that we,
>Being delivered from the hand of our enemies,
Might **serve** Him without fear,
>In holiness and righteousness before Him
>all the days of our life (Luke 1:74-75).

This continual practice of worship extends even beyond our lives on this earth. A lifestyle of worship will be the normal existence in heaven. John describes his vision of the citizens of heaven, who stand in God's presence, continually worshiping him: "Therefore they are before the throne of God, and **serve** Him day and night in His temple. And He who sits on the throne will dwell among them" (Revelation 7:15).

c. Worship is in the Holy Spirit
A lifestyle of worship is not possible without the power of the Holy Spirit. The apostle Paul writes, "For we are the circumcision, who **worship** God in the Spirit, rejoice in Christ Jesus, and have no confidence in the flesh" (Philippians 3:3). We cannot serve God in the flesh, but only in the Spirit. In a later section, we will discuss more fully what it means to worship "in Spirit and in Truth." We will explain the function of the Gifts of the Spirit within a worship service. Here, however, it is enough to observe that the everyday lifestyle of worship is made possible because the Holy Spirit strengthens and inspires us.

d. Worship is a response to forgiveness
The lifestyle of worship is in response to the "mercies of God" that have been bestowed upon us (Romans 12:1). The mercy of God and the forgiveness that we experience are benefits that flow out of the grace of God. We read in the book of Hebrews, "Therefore, since we are receiving a kingdom which cannot be shaken, let us have grace, by which we may **serve** God acceptably with reverence and godly fear" (Hebrews 12:28). Mercy, grace, and forgiveness produce in us a clean conscience, which gives us the inner liberty to worship God freely: "how much more shall the blood of Christ, who through the eternal Spirit offered Himself without spot to God, cleanse your conscience from dead works to **serve** the living God?" (Hebrews 9:14). The apostle Paul states further, "I thank God, whom I **serve** with a pure conscience, as my forefathers did,

as without ceasing I remember you in my prayers night and day" (2 Timothy 1:3).

e. Worship corresponds to the gospel of Jesus Christ

The forgiveness that we experience and the clean conscience that results from it are found in the gospel of Jesus Christ. In general, our lifestyle of worship is directed toward God; but, more specifically, our worship is part of our witness. As we serve God, we are also serving the gospel of Jesus. Paul makes this claim: "For God is my witness, whom I **serve** with my spirit in the gospel of His Son, that without ceasing I make mention of you always in my prayers" (Romans 1:9). Paul adds that his worship is Christian worship. He writes, "But this I confess to you, that according to the Way which they call a sect, so I **worship** the God of my fathers, believing all things which are written in the Law and in the Prophets" (Acts 24:14). When Paul says that he worships "according to the Way," he is speaking about the Christian faith. If we do not worship in accordance to the Way of Christ, then our worship is worthless. For example, Jesus accused the Pharisees of engaging in worthless worship because they worshiped according to human teaching and not in accord with divine revelation: "And in vain they **worship** Me, Teaching as doctrines the commandments of men" (Matthew 15:9).

f. Worshipers receive a heavenly reward

A lifestyle of worship is the most joyful and fulfilling kind of life. We walk continually in fellowship with God. True worship also leads to eternal blessings. The apostle Paul states, "knowing that from the LORD you will receive the reward of the inheritance; for you **serve** the LORD Christ" (Colossians 3:24). Clearly, if we "serve the LORD Christ" we will receive a reward on the day of judgment.

2. Fear: An attitude of worship

The New Testament concept of fearing God is essentially the same as the Old Testament concept. The fear of God (Greek *phobeomai*) is an attitude of honor, awe, and reverence towards God. This attitude of awe is essential to true worship.

a. Fearing God is a natural reaction to miracles

On one occasion, Jesus healed a man who was paralyzed. The people who saw the miracle were filled with awe. Luke tells us, "And they were all amazed, and they glorified God and were filled with **fear**, saying, 'We have seen strange things today!'" (Luke 5:26). The same result transpired when Jesus raised a young man from the dead. He interrupted the funeral and commanded the young man to rise up. Luke relates the rest of the story, "So he who was dead sat up and began to speak. And He presented him to his mother. Then **fear** came upon all, and they glorified God, saying, 'A great prophet has risen up among us;' and, 'God has visited His people'" (Luke 7:15-16). If we would pray and fast for miracles to happen in our churches, then deeper and more sincere worship would be the result.

b. Fearing God leads to church growth

When the people of God have an attitude of worship, they exert a powerful influence on the world around them. The book of Acts describes the attitudes and experiences of the early church. Luke writes, "Then the churches throughout all Judea, Galilee, and Samaria had peace and were edified. And walking in the **fear** of the LORD and in the comfort of the Holy Spirit, they were multiplied" (Acts 9:31). The believers had an attitude of worshipful respect in combination with the "comfort of the Holy Spirit," and this combination caused the churches to be multiplied. We are always looking for new methods of church growth, but true worship in the fear of God will produce growth.

c. Fearing God should be universal

In John's vision of the last days, he sees an angel

> flying in the midst of heaven, having the everlasting gospel to preach to those who dwell on the earth – to every nation, tribe, tongue, and people – saying with a loud voice, "**Fear** God and give glory to Him, for the hour of His judgment has come; and worship Him who made heaven and earth, the sea and springs of water" (Revelation 14:6-7).

The message of the angel is directed to every person on the face of the earth, and his message is threefold. He proclaims that everyone should 1. fear God, 2. give glory to God, and 3. worship God. These are three elements of the human response to God, our creator. Because God made heaven and earth, the sea and the springs, we should have an inner attitude of fear, honor, respect, and awe. Because God is creator, we should live a lifestyle that gives glory to God in everything that we do. Because God is a righteous judge, we should worship him with acts of praise and thanksgiving. God is worthy.

3. Bowing down: Actions of worship

The New Testament teaches that worship is a lifestyle of commitment to God and that worship is an attitude of awe and respect toward God. It also teaches that worship should be expressed in specific actions. Two Greek words are used to convey the actions of worship. The root meaning of the word *proskuneo* is "to put one's face to the ground, to pay homage." In its broader application, it means "to pay homage, to worship, to bow in adoration." The second word is *leitourgeo*, which means "to perform acts of worship." Both *proskuneo* and *leitourgeo* are used in reference to any act of worship that pays homage to God and that expresses veneration to God. These acts include prayers, songs, music, preaching, giving, and praise. They may refer to any intentional expression of praise or thanksgiving, whether in private or in public.

a. Worship is both an action and a lifestyle

Some people believe that a lifestyle that glorifies God is more important than the actions of worship, such as going to church. However, the Bible teaches that both are necessary. Jesus combines the two elements of worship into one statement. In the wilderness, Satan tempted Jesus, saying, "All these things I will give You if You will fall down and worship me" (Matthew 4:9). Jesus responded, saying, "Away with you, Satan! For it is written, 'You shall **worship** (*proskuneo*) the LORD your God, and Him only you shall **serve** (*latreuo*)'" (Matthew 4:10). Satan desired that Jesus would fall down and worship him, but Jesus refused. Jesus would not **worship** (*proskuneo*) Satan, which means that he would neither bow down nor offer any acts of homage. Also, Jesus would not

serve (*latreuo*) Satan, which means he would not make a commitment to live for Satan.

b. Worship may require considerable effort

Today's churches follow a schedule that makes worship convenient for everyone. We are concerned that if attending worship is too difficult, then people will not show up. However, people who value the experience of worship will do whatever is necessary to find a place to worship. When Jesus was born, wise men came hundreds of miles, traveling in caravans of camels and donkeys, to see Jesus and to worship him. When they arrived in Israel, they said, "Where is He who has been born King of the Jews? For we have seen His star in the East and have come to **worship** Him" (Matthew 2:2). If worship is important to us, then we will make the time to worship, and we will find a place to worship. We will enter into God's presence with praise and thanksgiving. We will always encounter challenges and hindrances, but we must not make excuses. We must worship Jesus.

c. Worship is the proper way to approach God in prayer

Just as some people separate worship and preaching as two distinct activities, some people think of prayer and worship as two separate activities. However, the Bible shows that prayer should be included as a part of worship. For example, when the ministry of Jesus became well known, many people came to him for healing and deliverance. On one occasion, "a leper came and **worshiped** Him, saying, 'LORD, if You are willing, You can make me clean'" (Matthew 8:2). The leper made his request within the context of worship. The apostle Paul seems to have had the same thing in mind when he wrote to the Philippian church and said to them, "Be anxious for nothing, but in everything by prayer and supplication, **with thanksgiving**, let your requests be made known to God" (Philippians 4:6). Prayer and worship belong together as two sides of the same coin. They are two aspects of our communion with God, two expressions of our relationship with God, two ways that demonstrate our love for God.

d. Worship must be in Spirit and in Truth

We saw earlier that a lifestyle of serving God can only be accomplished as the Holy Spirit gives us strength and direction. Similarly, our acts of worship can only be genuine when the Holy Spirit inspires us. Jesus said, "God is Spirit, and those who **worship** Him must **worship** in spirit and truth" (Jn. 4:24). We must pray in the Spirit (Jude 20; Ephesians 6:18); we must sing in the Spirit (Ephesians 5:18-19); we must preach in the Spirit (1 Corinthians 2:4); and we must rejoice in the Spirit (Luke 10:21). Every act of worship must be directed and empowered by the Holy Spirit. We will discuss this aspect of worship in more detail in a later section.

e. Worship is the continual occupation of heaven's inhabitants

Although this book is written to encourage the Church on the earth to worship God, we should be motivated by the fact that worship is the ongoing activity of everyone in heaven. John was taken up into heaven, and this is what he saw:

> the twenty-four elders fall down before Him who sits on the throne and **worship** Him who lives forever and ever, and cast their crowns before the throne, saying:
> You are worthy, O LORD,
> To receive glory and honor and power;
> For You created all things,
> And by Your will they exist and were created
> (Revelation 4:10-11).

John sees a vision of the twenty-four elders, representing the twelve tribes of Israel and the twelve apostles of Jesus, as they worship God. They speak forth words of honor, praise, exaltation, and adoration. Because God is worthy, we worship him now; and we will continue to worship him in heaven.

f. Worship of idols is the mark of unbelievers

Unbelievers also worship, but they do not worship God. John speaks about the people who refuse the gospel, saying, "So they **worshiped** the dragon who gave authority to the beast; and they **worshiped** the beast, saying, 'Who is like the beast? Who is able to make war with him?'" (Revelation 13:4). Unbelievers worship power, riches, and pleasure. The Church should be very careful that we do not fall into the trap of worshiping these idols.

g. Worship is the destiny of all nations

We learned earlier that all of the nations are destined to "serve" God by submitting to his authority. John tells us, furthermore, that all nations will fall down before God and perform acts of worship. He writes,

> Who shall not fear You, O LORD, and glorify Your name? For You alone are holy. For all nations shall come and **worship** before You, For Your judgments have been manifested (Revelation 15:4).

Perhaps John's vision of the future is a fulfillment of the prophecy of Isaiah 45:23 that is quoted and expanded by the apostle Paul: "at the name of Jesus every knee should bow, of those in heaven, and of those on earth, and of those under the earth, and that every tongue should confess that Jesus Christ is LORD, to the glory of God the Father" (Philippians 2:10-11).

h. Worship creates an environment where the Holy Spirit will speak

Not only does the Holy Spirit inspire our worship and direct our worship, but the Holy Spirit will reveal the will of God to us when we worship. We read in the book of Acts that several of the New Testament prophets and teachers had gathered together at the church in Antioch. Luke informs us, "As they **ministered** to the LORD and fasted, the Holy Spirit said, 'Now separate to Me Barnabas and Saul for the work to which I have called them'" (Acts 13:2). The word translated here as "ministered" is *leitourgeo*, the same word that is translated elsewhere as "worship." As we pointed out earlier, *leitourgeo* means "to perform acts of worship," and it is used in reference to any intentional act of worship. In this passage, the prophets and teachers were worshiping in conjunction with a time of fasting. No doubt their worship included singing, praying, and reading Scripture.

This combination of sincere worship along with fasting created a powerful setting for the Spirit to work. The Holy Spirit spoke either through a prophetic word or through tongues and interpretation to call Saul and Barnabas into missionary service. The other apostles obeyed the voice of the Spirit and commissioned Saul and Barnabas immediately. If we expect the Holy Spirit to speak in our services, we must worship God wholeheartedly. True worship opens the windows of heaven, so that the Spirit can move among us and speak to us.

D. A biblical definition of worship

Our study of biblical terminology leads to the conclusion that worship is expressed in three interrelated concepts: 1. Worship is ALLEGIANCE: Worship is a way of life, a commitment to God; 2. Worship is an ATTITUDE: Worship is an inner disposition of love, fear, and reverence; and 3. Worship is an ACTION: Worship is expressed through specific acts that show our gratitude to God and our esteem for him. As allegiance, worship is our day-by-day devotion to God, expressed in every aspect of our lives. As an attitude, worship is our humble acknowledgement of God's worthiness. As an action, worship includes all the ways that we honor God and all the ways that we express our love to God. All three of these elements make up the total worship of the Christian. True worship must involve a worshipful lifestyle, a worshipful heart, and worshipful actions. One without the others is less than God deserves and desires. Therefore, I would define true worship in the following way:

True worship is giving God the honor and esteem that is due to him as God. True worship is expressed through the believer's allegiance, attitudes, and actions.

Questions for Review and Application

1. What is the purpose of Chapter 2 of this book?

2. Which definition of worship do you find most accurate and helpful?

3. List and define the three primary Old Testament terms that are translated 'worship'.

4. Explain how serving God is a choice and how it is absolute.

5. Describe the role of the heart and the role of the will in our worship.

6. What makes worship joyful?

7. Can we enter heaven if we claim to believe in Christ, yet we are not worshipers of God? Explain.

8. Explain how worship as a lifestyle is different from worship as an attitude.

9. Write out a Bible verse that shows fearing God as a response to grace.

10. Why do you think the Israelites were tempted to fear the gods of Canaan?

11. Discuss how fearing God is related to loving God.

12. List seven acts of worship.

13. Using Abraham as an example, explain how all worship involves giving.

14. List three occasions in which worship was a response to answered prayer.

15. Name five Canaanite practices that were not allowed in Israelite worship.

16. What role did worship play in the lives of David and Job when they faced tragedy?

17. Name four actions of worship described in 1 Chronicles 16:23-31.

18. Explain the role of worship in producing victory.

19. What is the connection between worship and the reading of Scripture?

20. Define two New Testament words that demonstrate the lifestyle of worship.

21. Expound what Paul means when he says that we should present our "bodies a living sacrifice" which is our "reasonable service".

22. Clarify what is meant by worship as a response to grace and in correspondence to the gospel.

23. Describe the connection between miracles and worship.

24. Define the two Greek words that are used in reference to the acts of worship.

25. Explain how worship creates an environment in which the Holy Spirit speaks to us.

26. What is the author's definition of worship?

CHAPTER 3

THE OBJECT AND PURPOSE OF TRUE WORSHIP

This people I have formed for Myself; They shall declare My praise (Isaiah 43:21).

We have learned that true worship consists of a lifestyle, an attitude, and actions that give honor and glory to God. In this chapter we will expand our understanding of worship by discussing the object of our worship, the purposes and goals of worship, the impact of Pentecostal worship, hindrances to worship, and differences in worship.

A. The Object of our worship

1. Everyone worships something

Everyone worships something. If they do not worship Jehovah God, then they worship another god, or they worship idols. Modern idols often come in the form of materialism, pleasure, science, or the love of oneself. Whatever we love the most becomes a god to us.

In the ancient world, the worship of many gods simultaneously was common. The worship of many gods is called polytheism. For example, we read in the book of Acts that Paul preached in the city of Athens, Greece, where he observed statues and monuments in honor of a variety of gods. He was grieved when "he saw that the city was given over to idols" (Acts 17:16). Paul noticed that there was even an altar devoted to "THE UNKNOWN GOD" (Acts 17:23).

From within the ancient world, where everyone worshiped multiple gods, the LORD called out his people to be different. To Israel the LORD said, "You shall have no other gods before Me ... You shall not make for yourself a carved image ... you shall not bow down to them nor serve them. For I, the LORD your God, am a jealous God" (Deuteronomy 5:7-9). Our worship is very important to God, and he commands that we worship only him. Other gods are not allowed.

Many Christians mistakenly believe that they can worship God on Sunday and then serve other gods from Monday through Saturday. Such behavior is an abomination to God, and he considers it to be idolatry. As we learned in Chapter 2, God requires a lifestyle of complete devotion.

2. Christians worship only Jehovah, the God of the Bible

The worship of Jehovah alone is completely logical. There are good reasons for worshiping him alone. God does not demand our exclusive attention because he is in competition with other gods. There is no competition because the other gods are not truly God. The LORD spoke through prophet Isaiah, saying,

And there is no other God besides Me,
     A just God and a Savior;
     There is none besides Me (Isaiah 45:21).

The apostle Paul explains the reasons why we worship only Jehovah. He writes to the Colossian church:

giving thanks to the Father who has qualified us to be partakers of the inheritance of the saints in the light. He has delivered us from the power of darkness and conveyed us into the kingdom of the Son of His love, in whom we have redemption through His blood, the forgiveness of sins. He is the image of the invisible God, the firstborn over all creation. For by Him all things were created that are in heaven and that are on earth, visible and invisible, whether thrones or dominions or principalities or powers. All things were created through Him and for Him. And He is before all things, and in Him all things consist. And He is the head of the body, the church, who is the beginning, the firstborn from the dead, that in all things He may have the preeminence (Colossians 1:12-18).

a. Worship of Jehovah includes worship of Jesus

The first thing that we observe about Paul's powerful exhortation, is that he combines worship of the Father with worship of the Son. Paul begins by saying that we worship the Father because he has made us "partakers" of the benefits of salvation (v. 12) by delivering us out of the kingdom of darkness and placing us in the kingdom of his Son (v. 13). At this point, Paul proceeds to encourage the worship of Jesus. Jesus has "preeminence" (v. 18), which means he is worshiped as God. The reason we worship Jesus as God is because Jesus "is the image of the invisible God" (v. 15), because he is our redeemer (v. 14), because he created all things (v. 16), because he is the head of the Church (v. 18), and because he rose from the dead (v. 18)!

The importance of our worship of Jesus is confirmed by other Scriptures. The writer of Hebrews declares that when God sent Jesus into the world, he said, "Let all the angels of God **worship** Him" (Hebrews 1:6). Furthermore, when Jesus was born, the magi came from the East, "And when they had come into the house, they saw the young Child with Mary His mother, and fell down and **worshiped** Him. And when they had opened their treasures, they presented gifts to Him: gold, frankincense, and myrrh" (Matthew 2:11). During his earthly ministry, Jesus was worshiped on many occasions. For example, when Jesus walked on the water, "those who were in the boat came and **worshiped** Him, saying, 'Truly You are the Son of God'" (Matthew 14:33). Jesus was worshiped after his resurrection: "And as they went to tell His disciples, behold, Jesus met them, saying, 'Rejoice!' So they came and held Him by the feet and **worshiped** Him" (Matthew 28:9). The apostle Paul tells us that the day will come when "at the name of Jesus every knee should bow, of those in heaven, and of those on earth, and of those under the earth" (Philippians 2:10). John's Apocalypse reveals that Jesus is worshiped in heaven. All the hosts of heaven give honor and praise to the Lamb of God:

> And they sang a new song, saying:
> You are worthy to take the scroll,

And to open its seals;
For You were slain,
    And have redeemed us to God by Your blood
Out of every tribe and tongue and people and nation,
    And have made us kings and priests to our God;
    And we shall reign on the earth.

Then I looked, and I heard the voice of many angels around the throne, the living creatures, and the elders; and the number of them was ten thousand times ten thousand, and thousands of thousands, saying with a loud voice:

Worthy is the Lamb who was slain
    To receive power and riches and wisdom,
    And strength and honor and glory and blessing!"

And every creature which is in heaven and on the earth and under the earth and such as are in the sea, and all that are in them, I heard saying:

Blessing and honor and glory and power
    Be to Him who sits on the throne,
    And to the Lamb, forever and ever!

Then the four living creatures said, "Amen!" And the twenty-four elders fell down and **worshiped** Him who lives forever and ever (Revelation 5:9-14).

The exhortation of Paul and the worship of heaven reveal the sound reasons why we worship only the LORD.

b. We worship Jehovah because he is creator of all things
Paul states that we worship only Jehovah because he alone is the creator of all things (Colossians 1:16). King David declared that "all the gods of the peoples are idols, but the LORD made the heavens" (1 Chronicles 16:26; Psalm 96:5). No other god has the power of creation. The first verse of our Bible states unequivocally, "In the beginning God created the heavens and the earth" (Genesis 1:1). The prophet Isaiah proclaims that Jehovah is creator:

Have you not known?
    Have you not heard?
The everlasting God, the LORD,
    The Creator of the ends of the earth,

Neither faints nor is weary.

His understanding is unsearchable (Isaiah 40:28).

The apostle Paul asserts that the LORD created all things and continues to give life to all living things. He says, "God, who made the world and everything in it, since He is LORD of heaven and earth, does not dwell in temples made with hands. Nor is He worshiped with men's hands, as though He needed anything, since He gives to all life, breath, and all things" (Acts 17:24-25). Jehovah is neither confined to a temple, nor dependent upon any human action.

The worship of the LORD as creator extends, of course, to Jesus Christ, who participated with the Father and with the Holy Spirit in the act of creation. We might take note of the wording in Genesis 1: "In the beginning God (Father) created the heavens and the earth … and the Spirit of God (Holy Spirit) was hovering over the face of the waters. Then God said (the Word), 'Let there be light'" (Genesis 1:1-3). In light of the fact that Jesus is the Word, the Trinity is clearly present at creation. Jesus as the Word of creation is emphasized in the Gospel of John, when John writes, "In the beginning was the Word, and the Word was with God, and the Word was God. He was in the beginning with God. All things were made through Him, and without Him nothing was made that was made" (John 1:1-3).

We worship God because only God is the creator of all things. Only God is the beginning of all things. Only God can bring light out of darkness. Only God can make all things new. God's power of creation is the same power that makes us new creatures in Christ Jesus (2 Corinthians 5:17). Paul explains, "For it is the God who commanded light to shine out of darkness, who has shone in our hearts to give the light of the knowledge of the glory of God in the face of Jesus Christ: (2 Corinthians 4:6). This leads us to the second reason that we worship only Jehovah God.

c. We worship Jehovah because he is our only savior

We started this section with Paul's letter to the Colossians, in which he says of God, "He has delivered us from the power of darkness and conveyed us into the kingdom of the Son of His love, in whom we have redemption through His blood, the forgiveness of sins" (Colossians 1:13-14). We worship Jehovah because he has "delivered" us. He sent his Son into the world to die for our sins. God is our only savior.

The Ten Commandments begin with the statement of God's identity as savior. The LORD says, "I am the LORD your God who brought you out of the land of Egypt, out of the house of bondage" (Deuteronomy 5:6). Israel's worship of Jehovah is based upon the fact that he delivered them from Egyptian bondage. That basis for worship is repeated in 2 Kings 17:35-36):

> You shall not fear other gods, nor bow down to them nor serve them nor sacrifice to them; but the LORD, who brought you up from the land of Egypt with great power and an outstretched arm, Him you shall fear, Him you shall worship, and to Him you shall offer sacrifice.

Over and over, the LORD identifies himself as our savior. We read in the book of Isaiah, "I, even I, am the LORD, And besides Me there is no savior" (Isaiah 43:11). Again he says, "I, the LORD, am your Savior And your Redeemer, the Mighty One of Jacob" (Isa. 60:16).

Only Jehovah has the power to save. We may give our time and devotion to the gods of this world, but when we call upon them, they cannot help us nor save us (Isaiah 46:6-7).

3. Illegitimate objects of worship

We have already stated that the worship of idols is forbidden; however, idolatry takes many forms. At this point we will examine a few specific biblical texts that clarify the topic of idolatry.

a. We do not worship created things

Both in the ancient world and today, the worship of created things represents one form of idolatry. For example, the Egyptians worshiped the sun, the moon, and a variety of animals. Such worship is forbidden by Jehovah, who says, "And take heed, lest you lift your eyes to heaven, and when you see the sun, the moon, and the stars, all the host of heaven, you feel driven to **worship** them and serve them, which the LORD your God has given to all the peoples under the whole heaven as a heritage" (Deuteronomy 4:19). The

LORD explains further, saying, "You shall not make for yourself a carved image – any likeness of anything that is in heaven above, or that is in the earth beneath, or that is in the water under the earth; you shall not bow down to them nor **serve** them. For I, the LORD your God, am a jealous God" (Deuteronomy 5:6-9).

The apostle Paul points to immoral unbelievers in his day who refused to recognize God's authority. He describes them as people "who exchanged the truth of God for the lie, and **worshiped** and served the creature rather than the Creator" (Romans 1:25). Even today, religions such as Hinduism continue to venerate animals as gods. Hinduism, Taoism, Shinto, and some forms of Buddhism still retain some remnants of star worship. The modern New Age Movement also practices the worship of the sun and moon. Although western religions do not worship created things, our pursuit of money and pleasure would fit into Paul's description of idolatry as found in Romans 1. We might also consider the modern fixation on youth, physical beauty, and athletic prowess as forms of creature worship.

b. We do not worship angels

The worship of angels was apparently a concern in New Testament times. The Jews considered the angels to be just a bit lower than God; therefore, they were tempted to exalt the angels. The apostle Paul speaks in opposition to angel worship when he writes, "Let no one cheat you of your reward, taking delight in false humility and **worship** of angels, intruding into those things which he has not seen, vainly puffed up by his fleshly mind" (Colossians 2:18).

The appearance of angels can be so impressive, that humans automatically fall down to worship them. Even John, the writer of the Apocalypse, fell down to worship the angel who spoke with him: "And I fell at his feet to **worship** him. But he said to me, 'See that you do not do that! I am your fellow servant, and of your brethren who have the testimony of Jesus. **Worship** God!'" (Revelation 19:10). We read again later: "Now I, John, saw and heard these things. And when I heard and saw, I fell down to **worship** before the feet of the angel who showed me these things. Then he said to me, 'See that you do not do that. For I am your fellow servant, and of your brethren the prophets, and of those who keep the words of this book. **Worship** God'" (Revelation 22:8). Angels are more powerful than humans, but angels are only servants like us. They are not gods.

c. We do not worship demons

God gave command to the Israelites, saying, "They shall no more offer their sacrifices to demons, after whom they have played the harlot. This shall be a statute forever for them throughout their generations" (Leviticus 17:7). In the Apocalypse, John reports that after God sends various judgments upon the earth, some people do not repent of their worship of demons: "But the rest of mankind, who were not killed by these plagues, did not repent of the works of their hands, that they should not **worship** demons, and idols of gold, silver, brass, stone, and wood, which can neither see nor hear nor walk" (Revelation 9:20).

d. We do not worship ministers

Ministers of God should be respected and honored on account of their calling, but they should not be worshiped. Although ministers speak the Word of God, represent the gospel, and sometimes are the catalyst for miracles, they should not be worshiped. It is God who gives the minister the authority for preaching, praying, and believing (Acts 3:12-13).

For example, when the apostle Paul was bitten by a viper and did not die, the people believed that he was a god: "However, they were expecting that he would swell up or suddenly fall down dead. But after they had looked for a long time and saw no harm come to him, they changed their minds and said that he was a god" (Acts 28:6). Paul, however, was just a man – a man that trusted God for his healing.

The apostle Peter also experienced a case in which he was worshiped. The Holy Spirit directed Peter to go and preach the gospel at the house of a Roman centurion named Cornelius. "As Peter was coming in, Cornelius met him and fell down at his feet and **worshiped** him. But Peter lifted him up, saying, 'Stand up; I myself am also a man'" (Acts 10:25-26). Ministers should be careful to refuse any worship that is directed towards them. God does not share the glory, and he will judge those who allow themselves to be worshiped (See Acts 12:22-23).

B. The purposes and goals of worship

1. Corporate worship

Jehovah God (Father, Son, and Holy Spirit) is the only object of our worship. We have stated that true worship is giving the honor and glory to God that is due him as God. We also pointed out that worship is (1) a lifestyle, (2) an attitude, and (3) actions. From this point on, we will be focusing primarily on the third category, worship as actions. More specifically, we will give our attention to the activities that are included in the corporate worship of the Church. Our discussion of corporate worship, however, is not intended to devalue worship as a lifestyle and as an attitude. These two aspects of worship should always be present in the lives of the believers who gather in the Church.

In this section, we will expand on the definition of worship by talking about how corporate worship fits into the whole plan of God. What is the purpose of worship? What really constitutes the kind of worship that God wants? The purpose and goals of worship correspond to the purpose and goals of the Church, the Body of Christ. The three primary functions of the Church are 1. to worship God, 2. to disciple believers, and 3. to witness to the world. These three functions can be correlated to the three primary aims of worship: 1. True worship honors God. 2. True worship strengthens the Church. 3. True worship impacts the world.

2. True worship honors God

First and foremost, our worship is a way of honoring God. Worship is directed toward God; it is in praise of God; it is to honor God; it is to thank God; it is to lift up God. Worship is not worship unless it is honoring God. Otherwise, it is something else, but it is not worship. It may be music, it may be entertainment, it may be fellowship, but if it does not honor God, it is not worship.

Scripture teaches us that genuine worship glorifies God. The LORD describes the nature of his people: "This people I have formed for Myself; They shall declare My praise" (Isaiah 43:21).

The New Testament states a similar sentiment: "But you are a chosen generation, a royal priesthood, a holy nation, His own special people, that you may proclaim the praises of Him who called you out of darkness into His marvelous light" (1 Peter 2:9).

Honoring God is the number one focus of worship. We can broaden worship outside of the category of Sunday morning worship service or Wednesday night into the fact that we present our bodies a living sacrifice as a service of worship. Our very way of life from the time we get up in the morning until the time we go to bed at night is an offering of worship to the LORD. It is the giving of ourselves to the glory and honor of God, to the God who redeemed us, who brought us out of bondage; and therefore we give him our lives.

Thus, the primary purpose of worship is to exalt God, to praise God, and to adore God both for what he has done and for who he is. The purpose of worship is not to honor us, and it is not to honor our accomplishments. We do not worship so that we can boast in who we are. We do not worship to exalt our talents or to display our abilities. The purpose of worship is to honor God. That is why we are instructed to "make a joyful shout to the LORD" (Psalm 100:1). First and foremost, true worship must be focused upon God and not upon ourselves.

3. True worship strengthens the Church

Second, worship is an activity that builds up the Body of Christ. Throughout the Bible, we see that the faith community worships together. At first, families worshiped together; and when God formed the people of Israel, he called them together to worship. He instituted the tabernacle and all the rituals and liturgies of Israel. He emphasized the importance of worship as an activity of God's people together. Even when we worship in private, our worship is in companionship with the Church that is already in heaven. In the book of Hebrews we read,

> But you have come to Mount Zion and to the city of the living God, the heavenly Jerusalem, to an innumerable company of angels, to the general assembly and church of the firstborn

who are registered in heaven, to God the Judge of all, to the spirits of just men made perfect (Hebrews 12:22-23).

So much of the Church is already in heaven, and they stand before the throne of God, praising and worshiping God day and night (Revelation 7:15). When we praise God, even though we do not see the heavenly worship, we are in one spirit with the heavenly worship, so that our earthly worship is a mirror or a model of the heavenly worship. All of our worship is to be understood as a part of the Christian community.

Worship strengthens the Church through learning about God. In the book of 1 Corinthians, the apostle Paul speaks of worship as a means for the "edification" of the Church (1 Corinthians 14:3, 4, 5, 12, 17, 26). The word 'edify' means to build up, to strengthen. Worship, especially in the context of the Church, is not just focused on God and the individual, but it is an activity of God's people together. So that the worship that we engage in unites the body, shapes and forms the Body of Christ, and provides instruction. Even though worship is not primarily a teaching ministry; yet, people learn about God through worship. Think about a child that has been brought up in church. Consider how many songs, prayers, and testimonies they have heard, how many sermons and lessons they have heard about God. Worship teaches people about God.

Worship strengthens the Church by bringing people together. On any given Sunday, people who otherwise would not know each other come together as the Church. They enter the Church perhaps as strangers; but in a service of worship, they come together, and they sing together, and they pray together. As they worship together, they begin to form bonds of fellowship in the Body of Christ, and the Body of Christ is strengthened. Christianity is built on relationships – our relationship to God and our relationship with other believers. Although the propagation of the gospel by means of media is important, yet without personal fellowship and contact, we do not truly manifest the Body of Christ. People are lonely, and they need a family, and the family of God (the Church) can fill the need for belonging. God is glorified when his Body is being built up, when the Body of Christ is getting stronger, when the Body of Christ is growing in the unity of the faith. God is exalted when the

Body of Christ is discipling one another and testifying to one another.

Worship strengthens the Church for battle. When we come together, God begins to move, and the Spirit of the LORD is present. Then the house becomes a holy place, and people are built up, encouraged, and strengthened. The corporate worship of the Church can be likened to many different metaphors. It is like the training camp for a soldier. Soldiers are never sent out to battle until they are trained. The Church itself is not the battleground, but it is the training ground. The worship is the place where people are built up and strengthened for the battles that will emerge out in the world. Believers receive strength from being in God's presence with God's people. As we plan our worship services, we should aim for a worship service that encourages people, that builds up people, that brings people together, and that teaches people how to minister one to another in the Body of Christ.

4. True worship impacts the world

Third, inasmuch as the Church is located in the world, the Church exists as a witness; and worship is a part of our witness. Throughout the Bible, the people of God are called to be a witness to the world; and even though most of our witness occurs outside of the worship service, our worship should in some way impact the world and the community. As a witness to the world, our worship should show forth God's glory to those who are not Christians. Therefore, they see in us the grace of God, the love of God, the works of God, and the Word of God. The apostle Paul speaks about this in first Corinthians, when he says, if an unbeliever comes into your worship "he is convinced by all, he is convicted by all. And thus the secrets of his heart are revealed; and so, falling down on his face, he will worship God and report that God is truly among you" (1 Corinthians 14:24-25).

Therefore, our worship is a witness to the world, and it is only when we genuinely, truly worship God that the world will be impacted. The world is not impacted if our services are only entertainment, that is, if we are not truly worshiping. The world is not impacted if our worship does not display our Christian unity. The world is not impacted if we are preaching our own ideas instead of the Word of God. However, if we worship God truly, the world will receive our worship as a witness. The world is impacted by a church where God is exalted and where needs are met. The world is impacted by a worshiping church that is concerned about the local community and is involved in reaching out.

C. The impact of Pentecostal worship

Through its worship, the Pentecostal movement has radically transformed global Christianity in the last 100 years. Renowned theologian and historian Walter Hollenweger states that Pentecostalism's "most important contribution" to the larger Christian tradition has been its worship.[1] Other scholars have shown that worship is at the center of Pentecostalism's rapid growth around the world.[2] If our churches have stopped growing; then, perhaps it is because we have stopped worshiping. Worship touches the heart of God and opens up the worshiper to God's powerful presence. True worship attracts hungry souls like the warmth of a fire attracts a cold and weary traveler.

The theological heart of Pentecostalism states that Jesus is our savior, sanctifier, Spirit baptizer, healer, and soon coming king. All of these experiences take place within the context of worship. It is in the time of worship that people are saved, sanctified, baptized in the Spirit, healed, and filled with the hope of Christ's coming. Holding to our doctrines on paper is not enough – we must put them into practice if our movement is to have a future.

The Jews worshiped in Jerusalem, but the Samaritans worshiped on Mount Gerizim (John 4:20-23). The Samaritans accepted only the Pentateuch as the word of God, but the Jews accepted the entire Old Testament. These differences were part of what separated the Jews from the Samaritans. Similarly, the Pentecostal movement is different from Roman Catholicism or other

---

[1] Walter J. Hollenweger, *The Pentecostals: The Charismatic Movement in the Churches* (Minneapolis, MN: Augsburg Pub. House, 1st U.S. edn, 1972), p. 466.
[2] Donald E. Miller and Tetsunao Yamamori, *Global Pentecostalism: The New Face of Christian Social Engagement* (Berkeley, CA: University of California Press, 2007), p. 23.

denominations. Worship is at the heart of our Pentecostal identity. The power of our worship, the format of our worship, the spirit of our worship, and the place of our worship are what define us as a Pentecostal people. The songs that we sing, the prayers that we pray, the type of sermons that we preach, and the sacraments that we celebrate are important marks of our identity. If the Pentecostal movement is to continue, we must continue to emphasize Pentecostal worship that includes the moving of the Holy Spirit.

D. Hindrances to worship

We have argued that nothing is more important than our worship. If that is true, then why is it so difficult to get some people to worship? The answer is that although God is pleased when we worship him, our enemy (Satan) is envious of the glory that we give to God. Therefore, Satan fights against our worship and tries to take it unto himself. Satan uses the following tactics to hinder us from true worship.

1. Pride hinders us from worshiping God
Pride was the cause of Satan's downfall, and pride is the most dangerous enemy of true worship. Let us consider the words of the prophet Isaiah concerning the fall of Lucifer:

How you are fallen from heaven,
    O Lucifer, son of the morning!
How you are cut down to the ground,
    You who weakened the nations!
For you have said in your heart:
    "I will ascend into heaven,
I will exalt my throne above the stars of God;
    I will also sit on the mount of the congregation
    On the farthest sides of the north;
I will ascend above the heights of the clouds,
    I will be like the Most High."
Yet you shall be brought down to Sheol,
    To the lowest depths of the Pit (Isaiah 14:12-15).

Worship requires an attitude of humility. True worship requires that we acknowledge God as God. We must humbly admit that we are not God. We must confess that God is in control, and that we are not in control. We must humbly say that Jesus is LORD, and we are not LORD. Worship requires a humility that surrenders everything to the LORD. In true worship, we must surrender our arrogance, pride, self-reliance, and boastfulness. Worship requires that we admit that we need God, and that he is the Almighty. True worship humbly acknowledges that he is the creator and we are the creature.

2. Sin separates us from worship

While pride may be the greatest hindrance to worship, any kind of sin will damage our relationship with God. In order to worship God, we must be in fellowship with God. The recognition of sin in our lives makes us want to hide from God like Adam and Eve in the Garden (Genesis 3:8-10). Whenever we come near to God, our sin is revealed, and that makes us very uncomfortable. For example, when Isaiah found himself in the mighty presence of God, his first response was to think of his sinfulness. Isaiah said, "Woe is me, for I am undone! Because I am a man of unclean lips, And I dwell in the midst of a people of unclean lips; For my eyes have seen the King, The LORD of hosts" (Isaiah 6:5). The only solution to the problem of sin is to confess and repent of that sin like Isaiah did. If we confess our sins, God is "faithful and just to forgive us our sins and to cleanse us from all unrighteousness" (1 John 1:9). With our sins forgiven, we can enter humbly into God's presence and receive all the benefits of his grace. The psalmist David states the matter plainly:

> Who may ascend into the hill of the LORD?
>   Or who may stand in His holy place?
> He who has clean hands and a pure heart,
>   Who has not lifted up his soul to an idol,
>   Nor sworn deceitfully.
> He shall receive blessing from the LORD,
>   And righteousness from the God of his salvation
> (Psalm 24:3-5).

3. A False view of Christianity makes us undervalue worship

Unfortunately, some people view their conversion as a conclusion rather than a beginning. However, the New Testament uses the term "new birth" for a reason – because birth signifies a new start, a new beginning. The point of birth is not an end. Growth immediately follows birth. Our growth comes through the nurture of our ongoing relationship with God; and our relationship with God is largely dependent upon our lifestyle of worship, our attitude of worship, and our regular acts of worship. Christianity is more than a set of beliefs that Jesus died on the cross and rose from the dead. God expects a worshiping believer.

4. Some people have not been taught how to worship

Many believers do not truly worship because they simply do not know how to worship. Worship is something that must be learned. Many churches do not practice true worship; therefore, the church members do not have a model to follow. If the church is spiritually dead, then the people will not be taught how to worship. Worship is not a spectator sport – participation is required. Worship is not like a concert, a play, the theatre, or sports, where participation is optional. Every church should make it a priority to teach the youth and new converts how to worship God in Spirit and in Truth.

E. Differences in Worship

1. Styles of worship may be different

I have worshiped in twenty-seven different states within the USA, several churches in Korea, the Philippines, and Puerto Rico, one church in Ecuador, and one church in Haiti. I have worshiped in Soshanguve, South Africa. I have worshiped with different ethnic groups: Haitian, Korean, Filipino, various Latino groups, African-American, Jamaican, Romanian, and Native American. Worship in the Korean church is different from worship in the Filipino church, even though both churches are Asian. Worship in the Haitian church is different from worship in the South African church. Worship in Ecuador is different from worship in Puerto Rico, even though both churches speak Spanish. Worship in the African-American church is different from worship in the Jamaican church.

Worship in the Romanian church is different from worship in the Native American church. Each culture and ethnic group has its own unique style of worship, its own unique liturgy, and its own unique traditions concerning worship. These cultural differences should be appreciated and honored as valid expressions of true worship. God loves our worship, and it makes no difference to him if the worship is offered in German, English, Spanish, French, Cherokee, Zulu, or Japanese. We may worship with a tambourine, a flute, a piano, a pipe organ, a drum, or a trombone. We may sing, shout, leap, clap, or dance. Regardless of the cultural expression, God will receive and bless our worship if we worship in Spirit and in Truth.

2. Changing methods

Many changes are happening in the realm of worship. We need to ask ourselves if these changes are good or bad. One new style of worship has been created to accommodate what is called the Seeker Sensitive model of the Church. The Seeker Sensitive Church organizes the entire worship service in such a way that un-churched people will feel more comfortable and at home. It is an attempt to win new people to the Church by very gradually intro-ducing them to Christian ideas. As long as they remain faithful to the gospel, the Seeker Sensitive churches should be commended for their attempt to communicate the gospel clearly and simply. Too often, the Church speaks a language that unchurched people cannot understand and with which they cannot identify. The apos-tle Paul argues that we must adapt our methodology to meet the challenges within our culture. He writes,

> though I am free from all men, I have made myself a servant to all, that I might win the more; and to the Jews I became as a Jew, that I might win Jews; to those who are under the law, as under the law, that I might win those who are under the law; to those who are without law, as without law (not being without law toward God, but under law toward Christ), that I might win those who are without law; to the weak I became as weak, that I might win the weak. I have become all things to all men, that I might by all means save some. Now this I do for the gospel's sake (1 Corinthians 9:19-23).

The Seeker Sensitive model, however, has its weaknesses. For example, the confrontational element of the gospel cannot be eliminated. The gospel itself is "foolishness" to some people and a "stumblingblock" to others. Again, the apostle Paul writes,

> For the message of the cross is foolishness to those who are perishing, but to us who are being saved it is the power of God. For it is written: "I will destroy the wisdom of the wise, And bring to nothing the understanding of the prudent." Where is the wise? Where is the scribe? Where is the disputer of this age? Has not God made foolish the wisdom of this world? For since, in the wisdom of God, the world through wisdom did not know God, it pleased God through the foolishness of the message preached to save those who believe. For Jews request a sign, and Greeks seek after wisdom; but we preach Christ crucified, to the Jews a stumbling block and to the Greeks foolishness, but to those who are called, both Jews and Greeks, Christ the power of God and the wisdom of God. Because the foolishness of God is wiser than men, and the weakness of God is stronger than men (1 Corinthians 1:18-25).

Although Paul was willing to make concessions in order to communicate to the world around him, he recognized that the gospel itself makes people uncomfortable. When unbelievers enter our churches, we should welcome them and treat them with love and kindness. The worship, the praying, and the preaching, however, will produce conviction of sin within the heart of the unbeliever; and they will become uncomfortable. True worship does not give comfort to the wicked. God loves the sinner, but God desires the sinner to turn away from sin and to turn unto God.

Following the Seeker Sensitive Church movement came the Emergent Church movement. The Emergent Church downplays denominations and formalities. Everyone is encouraged to dress casually, and the preaching is presented in a conversational manner with a low-key tone. Once again, the style of the worship service appears to be more important than the theological content of the sermon and the songs.

After the Emergent Church came the Missional Church. The Missional Church seeks to reach outside the four walls of the church building and minister to the community. The Missional Church encourages every member to be a missionary in their community. It seems to me that the term "Missional Church" is just another label that describes what the true Church has always been. The Pentecostal church, for example, has always focused on mission. The baptism in the Holy Spirit has always produced mission. We read in the New Testament, "But you shall receive power when the Holy Spirit has come upon you; and you shall be witnesses to Me in Jerusalem, and in all Judea and Samaria, and to the end of the earth" (Acts 1:8); "And they went out and preached everywhere, the LORD working with them and confirming the word through the accompanying signs" (Mark 16:20).

Whether it be the Seeker Sensitive Church, the Emergent Church, or the Missional Church, we need to ask how these new perspectives affect our worship. In this book, I propose that worship style is not as important as worship substance. We may dress formally or we can dress casually. We may or may not have colored lights flashing. We may or may not serve coffee and doughnuts. We may preach in conversational tones or in a traditional preaching style. At the heart of our worship, however, we must focus on encountering the presence of God. We must celebrate with exuberant praises and shouts of victory. We must be certain to include time for prayer, which includes places for prayer where people are encouraged to be converted and filled with the Spirit. We must include space in our worship for praying for the sick. If we lose these things, we are no longer Pentecostal.

3. Worship conflicts

While there is no doubt that these intense worship wars are continuing to cause deep animosity among Christians and to divide churches, it would be a mistake to believe that these conflicts are new. Any significant change in worship styles has always produced friction. However, these changes are more noticeable at the present time because of the rapid pace of change. In the past, significant alteration of the Church's worship may have required half a century, but now we can experience major changes in the course of a few years.

a. Cain and Abel

To put our discussion into the proper context, let us be reminded that differing beliefs about worship have led to innumerable conflicts throughout history. In fact, the world's first murder was committed on account of a disagreement over what constituted acceptable worship. Cain and Abel, the first two sons of Adam and Eve, brought their offerings to the LORD. Cain brought an offering "of the fruit of the ground," and Abel "brought the firstborn of his flock". We read that "the LORD respected Abel and his offering, but He did not respect Cain and his offering. And Cain was very angry" (Genesis 4:3-5).

Many interpreters believe that God refused Cain's offering because it was not a blood sacrifice. If Cain did not have access to a lamb, he could have purchased one by trading his "fruit of the ground". He then could have offered the lamb to God. Other interpreters, however, have argued that God refused Cain's offering because Cain did not approach God with the proper attitude of humility, faith, and worship. It should be observed that grain offerings and drink offerings (from grapes) were a valid part of the Old Testament system of offerings (Exodus 29:41; Leviticus 2:1; 6:14; 23:13, etc.). Consequently, we might deduce that the content of Cain's offering was acceptable but that his worship was offered in the wrong spirit. In this vein, the writer of Hebrews declares that Abel's offering was presented "by faith", which made it a "more excellent sacrifice" than Cain's (Hebrews 11:4; see also 1 John 3:12 and Jude v. 11).

Even if we are not certain why Cain's worship was unacceptable to God, we know that God appeared to him and advised him how he could remedy the situation and how he could worship properly. The LORD told Cain that if he would submit the proper offering with the right attitude, then he would be accepted (Genesis 4:7). Cain, however, was not teachable and not willing to worship according to God's plan. Blind with jealousy against his brother Abel, Cain struck and killed him: "and it came to pass, when they were in the field, that Cain rose up against Abel his brother and killed him" (Genesis 4:8).

We learn from the story of Cain and Abel that God requires all worshipers to offer their worship according to God's standards. We are not free to invent our own worship practices outside of God's instructions. We also learn that when we are confronted by God's Word, we should be willing to conform to His will rather than to continue in our disobedience. Finally, we learn that disagreements over worship can lead to deep anger, divisions, and even violence between brothers.

b. King David

Another example of disagreement over worship began when King David decided to bring the Ark of the Covenant to Jerusalem. As David brought the Ark into the city with great jubilation and gladness, he "danced before the LORD with all his might; and David was wearing a linen ephod" (2 Samuel 6:14). All the people of Israel rejoiced along with David. We read that "David and all the house of Israel brought up the ark of the LORD with shouting and with the sound of the trumpet" (2 Samuel 6:15). However, David's wife Michal was not pleased to see David's bold display of worship. She saw him "leaping and whirling before the LORD; and she despised him in her heart" (2 Samuel 6:16). When David returned home, his wife Michal confronted him with her stinging criticism. She said,

> "How glorious was the king of Israel today, uncovering himself today in the eyes of the maids of his servants, as one of the base fellows shamelessly uncovers himself!" So David said to Michal, "It was before the LORD, who chose me instead of your father and all his house, to appoint me ruler over the people of the LORD, over Israel. Therefore I will play music before the LORD. And I will be even more undignified than this, and will be humble in my own sight. But as for the maidservants of whom you have spoken, by them I will be held in honor" (2 Samuel 6:20-22).

David had removed his royal robes and had worshiped with the common people. His humility had displeased Michal, and she accused him of being undignified. David replied that he would be even more undignified in the future and that he would continue to worship the LORD wholeheartedly. David insisted that the common people would esteem him highly for his humility in worship. Unfortunately, Michal's criticism did irreparable harm to her relationship with David, and she never had any children from the marriage. Disagreements over worship can cause permanent and painful hostilities, even within families.

c. Jesus and the Samaritan woman

Jesus found himself in the middle of a worship war when he encountered the Samaritan woman at Jacob's well. When Jesus asks her for a drink of water, her first response is to point out their differences. She is a Samaritan, and Jesus is a Jew; and the 'Jews have no dealings with the Samaritans' (John 4:9). Jesus, however, speaks to her about the need for living water. He also speaks to her personal situation, noting that she had been married five times. Realizing that Jesus was a prophet, she brings up their differences regarding their places of worship. The Jews worshiped in Jerusalem, but the Samaritans worshiped on Mount Gerizim. Jesus' response to her reveals that the location of worship is not God's ultimate concern. Jesus says, "Woman, believe Me, the hour is coming when you will neither on this mountain, nor in Jerusalem, worship the Father" (v. 21). In Chapter 6, we will look more deeply into Jesus' conversation with the Samaritan woman.

Jesus' words to the Samaritan woman imply that God is not pleased with all forms of worship. Some worship is not acceptable to God. As we mentioned above, the worship of Cain was not accepted by God. Also, Jesus warned the Pharisees, "These people draw near to Me with their mouth, and honor Me with their lips, but their heart is far from Me. And in vain they worship Me, teaching as doctrines the commandments of men" (Matthew 15:8-9). True worship comes from the heart, and if worship does not come from the heart, God does not accept it.

Questions for Review and Application

1. Explain the term 'polytheism'.

2. Read Isaiah chapter 45 and list four points found there regarding worship.

3. List four Bible verses that tell us why we should worship Jesus.

4. Demonstrate the role of the Trinity in creation.

5. Write out Isaiah 46:6-7.

6. Tell some ways in which we worship the creature rather than the creator.

7. Name two examples from the New Testament when people were tempted to worship angels.

8. Explain why people sometimes worship ministers.

9. Name the three primary functions of the Church.

10. Describe how true worship honors God.

11. Describe how true worship strengthens the Church.

12. Describe how true worship is a witness to the world.

13. What are three characteristics of Pentecostal worship?

14. Why does Satan try to hinder our worship?

15. How is pride opposed to true worship?

16. How do we prevent sin from hindering our worship?

17. Explain where worship fits into our relationship with God.

18. Share your own thoughts regarding ways to teach the youth how to worship God.

19. Name three new models for the Church.

20. What do you think caused the Lord to reject Cain's offering?

21. Why did David's wife Michal criticize his worship?

CHAPTER 4

ENCOUNTERING GOD THROUGH WORSHIP

Now it came to pass in the thirtieth year, in the fourth month, on the fifth day of the month, as I was among the captives by the River Chebar, that the heavens were opened and I saw visions of God (Ezekiel 1:1).

A. Encountering the presence of God

1. The expectancy of worship

When we gather for worship as the people of God, we expect to meet with one another and fellowship together. We expect to teach one another, encourage one another, pray for one another, and talk to one another about God. However, we expect something more; because Jesus promised, "where two or three are gathered together in My name, I am there in the midst of them" (Matthew 18:20).

When we gather to worship God, we expect to encounter the presence of God. Worship involves both the horizontal relationships (human to human) and the vertical relationship (human to God). The worship service is conducted in such a way that we not only talk to one another, but we also talk to God. We not only encourage one another, we also exalt and praise God. We not only listen to each other, we also listen to God. Without the presence of God, the worship service would be just another social gathering.

The prophet Isaiah was in the temple, worshiping the LORD, when he suddenly found himself encountering God in an extraordinary way. He "saw the LORD sitting on a throne, high and lifted up," and around the LORD there were seraphim flying to and fro crying out "Holy, holy, holy is the LORD of Hosts; The whole earth is full of His glory!" (Isaiah 6:1-3).

Isaiah was exposed to the transcendent awesomeness of God, and he was forever transformed by the experience. In the presence of God, Isaiah's sinfulness became unbearable. He confessed, and God cleansed him with a hot coal from the altar. Being in the presence of God made Isaiah want to be holy like God.

Although most of us will never have an experience like that of Isaiah, we can encounter God in many ways through worship. We can acknowledge that where two or three are gathered for worship, Jesus is in the midst. Like John on the island of Patmos, we can be "in the Spirit on the LORD's Day" (Revelation 1:10).

Inherent to Pentecostal worship is a hunger and thirst for the life-giving, transforming presence of God. Pentecostal theologian Daniel Albrecht states that the entire Pentecostal worship service "is aimed toward an *encounter*" with God;[1] and Jerome Boone claims that the "single most important goal of any Pentecostal worship service is a personal encounter with the Spirit of God."[2] When we encounter God, something wonderful and powerful will happen. The goal of worship is that every hearer will be filled with the Holy Spirit.

The book of Acts tells us about such a worship service. While Peter preached, the Holy Spirit fell on all those that heard the Word of God (Acts 10:44). Without warning and without planning, the Holy Spirit descended upon the people in a miraculous way. We cannot schedule the moving of the Holy Spirit, but we can pray for it and expect it. Suddenly, the Holy Spirit falls and we forget who we are, because we see who God is. We forget where we are, because God has said, "Come up here" (Revelation 4:1).

---

[1] Daniel E. Albrecht, "Pentecostal Spirituality: Looking through the Lens of Ritual," *Pneuma* 14.2 (1992), p. 110 (emphasis in the original).

[2] R. Jerome Boone, "Community and Worship: The Key Components of Pentecostal Christian Formation," *Journal of Pentecostal Theology* 8 (1996), p. 137.

2. The necessity of worship

We first encounter God in the experience of salvation. God comes to us, offering himself as our savior. The biblical pattern of salvation is Israel's exodus from Egypt. The Israelites found themselves in bondage in Egypt, and they cried out for deliverance. The LORD heard their cries; therefore, he appeared to Moses on the back side of the desert and said,

> I have surely seen the oppression of My people who are in Egypt, and have heard their cry because of their taskmasters, for I know their sorrows. So I have come down to deliver them out of the hand of the Egyptians, and to bring them up from that land to a good and large land, to a land flowing with milk and honey (Exodus 3:7-8).

Over the period of the next few weeks, the Israelites came to know God as their savior. The LORD sent ten plagues against the Egyptians until they were willing to let the Israelites go free.

The redeemed people of God crossed through the Red Sea and soon made their way to Mount Sinai, where they entered into the covenant with the LORD. In that covenant, the LORD established the ongoing method for the people to encounter God – in worship. God commanded them to build a tabernacle where they would meet with God on a regular basis.

The Old Testament books of Exodus and Leviticus provide detailed instructions for Israel's worship. They show that regular worship is essential for building unity and identity. It is in worship that God's people are reminded who they are and who God is. In worship, we remember God's mighty acts of salvation. Without this worship, God's people will be assimilated into the surrounding culture. Worship reminds us that although we are in the world, we are "not of the world" (John 17:15-18).

Worship in some ways is a reciting of the past. It is our testimony, telling of what God has done. But it needs to go beyond retelling the past. The ingredients in a worship service do more than just testify of the past; they recreate and represent the presence of God for today. It is not enough to know that God acted in the past; we must be able to see God's actions in the present. In worship, we remember God's work in the past, and we also encounter God in the present.

3. Encountering God in the feasts

The worship of Israel included three major festivals that were commemorations of God's previous acts of salvation. Each feast carried a special meaning: 1. The Passover commemorated the exodus from Egypt. 2. The Feast of Weeks (Pentecost) commemorated God's giving of the Covenant on Mount Sinai. 3. The Feast of Tabernacles commemorated Israel's journey through the wilderness.

Although the feasts were rooted in past events, they held deep significance for Israel's present view of God. The annual Passover ceremony is a reenactment and a retelling of the first Passover when the Israelites were still in Egypt. God destroyed the firstborn of Egypt, but he passed over the Israelites who sacrificed a lamb and placed its blood on the door. We see the Passover sacrifice as a prefiguring of the death of Christ. Jesus is the lamb that is slain, and it is his blood that is sprinkled. Yet, Passover also continues to have a present significance. We believe that Jehovah God, who brought up Israel out of Egypt, will save anyone today who calls upon him. The Passover shows us that "whoever calls on the name of the LORD Shall be saved" (Acts 2:21).

Fifty days after Passover, Israel celebrated the Feast of Weeks (Pentecost). It is associated with the giving of the covenant on Sinai and, in the New Testament, the giving of the Spirit. The present relevance of the Feast of Weeks is found in God's ongoing commitment to the New Covenant in Jesus Christ and in God's willingness to pour out his Holy Spirit upon all flesh. Jesus continues to bring people into the New Covenant, and God continues to fill hungry souls with the Spirit and power of Pentecost.

The Feast of Tabernacles commemorated the wilderness wanderings. God cared for Israel in the wilderness as they journeyed toward the Promised Land. He fed them with manna and brought water out of the rock. This feast teaches us that the Christian life is a journey in which God wants us to go forward with him in obedience and in faith (Hebrews 3:7-4:11). Like Israel in the wilderness, we are strangers and pilgrims in the earth (Hebrews 11:13).

4. The covenant community in worship

Although God deals with every person as an individual, his covenant is with his whole people of God in community. The corporate nature of the covenant includes the necessity of corporate worship where we gather together to respond to God's revelation. The covenant is a relationship, and it is represented in the Bible by the symbol of marriage. Therefore, the Church is the Bride of Christ. Worship is an expression of our covenant commitment to God, and our praises are in response to God's covenant faithfulness.

Mutual commitment is the heart of the covenant; and is, therefore, the foundation of genuine worship. The LORD is fully committed to us, and we are fully committed to the LORD. The LORD promises to be present, "enthroned in the praises of Israel" (Psalm 22:4); and just as every Israelite was required to be present at the Tabernacle/Temple, every New Testament believer is required to be present in worship.

B. Encountering God in the worship of the tabernacle

Israel's worship took place in the Tabernacle, which was later replaced by the Jerusalem Temple. The Tabernacle was a large tent that sat within a fenced courtyard. The inside of the tent was divided into two parts: (1) the Holy Place, which contained a table for bread, an altar for incense and a lampstand; and (2) the holy of holies, a smaller and more sacred division where the Ark of the Covenant rested. Within the courtyard outside the tent stood the main altar and the laver. Priests were active in the courtyard section, offering sacrifices and meeting with the people. Access to the Holy Place was limited, and entry into the Holy of Holies was permitted only one day a year to the high priest.

We can learn something about the nature of true worship from the three primary names that were given to the Tabernacle. These names are (1) the Tent of Meeting, (2) the Sanctuary, and (3) the Tabernacle.

1. The Tent of Meeting

First, the Tabernacle was called the "Tent of Meeting," (Hebrew, *ohel moed*), a name that designates the purpose of the structure.

There at the Tent of Meeting (mentioned 108 times), God would meet together with his people. There, the people's priestly representatives would meet with the LORD. At the door of the Tent of Meeting, the dispute between Moses, Aaron, and Miriam was arbitrated (Numbers 12:4). Lambs were offered as sacrifices every morning and every evening at the door of the Tent of Meeting (Exodus 29:39-41). At the door to the Tent of Meeting, said the LORD, "I will meet you to speak with you" (Exodus 29:42). The entire contents of the book of Leviticus are represented as being delivered to Moses by the LORD at the door of the Tent of Meeting (Leviticus 1:1). As the name implies, the tent of meeting was the place where the LORD and his people would meet.

Regarding worship, the Tent of Meeting signifies that there are appointed times when we meet with God, and there are appointed places where we meet with God. As New Testament believers, we know that God is present everywhere, and that we can meet with him at any time and at any place. However, we still read in the New Testament that we should not "forsake the assembling" of ourselves together as the Church (Hebrews 10:25). We read that it was the custom of Jesus and of Paul to attend worship services (Luke 4:16; Acts 17:2). We are told that the early Church met for worship on Sundays (1 Corinthians 16:2). The Tent of Meeting emphasizes that there is a time and a place for God's people to meet together to worship God.

2. The Tabernacle

The second name for this worship structure was "Tabernacle" (Hebrew *mishkan*). The word Tabernacle means "dwelling place," and it is mentioned 139 times. The LORD instructed Moses to build the Tabernacle for Israel so that the LORD could "dwell in their midst' (Exodus 25:8). The LORD explained further, "I will set My tabernacle among you, and My soul shall not abhor you. I will walk among you and be your God, and you shall be My people" (Leviticus 26:11-12).

The word 'Tabernacle,' therefore, emphasizes that Jehovah God has promised to "dwell" with his people forever. To dwell signifies the active sense of living with them. When the tabernacle was completed, the LORD descended upon the Tabernacle in the glory cloud as a sign that he had come now to inhabit it (Exodus 40:34-38). Through their journey in the wilderness, the cloud had been evidence of the LORD's presence. But now, the presence of the LORD entered into the Tabernacle and made it God's permanent residence. The Ark of the Covenant reinforced the fact that the LORD resided there. The Ark represented the throne of God in the Holy of Holies.

Regarding worship, the Tabernacle signifies God's continual presence among his people (Revelation 1:13). God does not come and go; he abides with us always. The Tabernacle represents God's nearness. Although we realize that he cannot be contained within a tent or building, God chooses to call the Tabernacle his home. He is present at all times. He never leaves the Tabernacle. We can depend upon the fact that God is always present. To borrow from the language of the psalmist, "God is our refuge and strength, A very present help in trouble" (Psalm 46:1). Moses was able to say, "For what great nation is there that has God so near to it, as the LORD our God is to us" (Deuteronomy 4:7).

3. The Sanctuary

A third designation for the Tabernacle is "sanctuary" (Hebrew *miqdash*). This term is derived from the Hebrew root *qadosh*, which means "holy." The Sanctuary is a holy place, and it reinforces the notion of holiness or separateness for God and for his people. The holiness of the Sanctuary is further witnessed by the head covering of the high priest, which was engraved with the words "Holiness to the LORD" (Exodus 28:36). God instructed the people, saying, "You shall ... reverence My sanctuary: I am the LORD" (Leviticus 26:2). The designation of the Tabernacle as a Sanctuary suggests that God is unapproachable and distant, that he is "high and lifted up" (Isaiah 6:1). The Sanctuary was not an ordinary building – it was set apart for Jehovah and special to him.

Regarding worship, the Sanctuary emphasizes that God is holy; therefore, he is worthy of our worship. God is exalted above all things, and the Sanctuary should be treated with the utmost of respect and reverence. The Sanctuary is holy because God dwells there. Even the very ground is holy when God is present (Exodus 3:5). Entering the Sanctuary reminds us that worship should not be taken lightly. Worship is joyful but not frivolous. Worship can be spontaneous but not careless or disorderly.

4. God is high and lifted up, but God is also near us

The names for the Tabernacle illustrate the contrast between God's nearness and God's separateness from us. The fact that God is close at hand, involved in our lives, and available when we pray is what theologians call his **immanence**. To say that God is immanent means that he dwells with us and cares about us. However, God is also holy, separate, and awesome. These are qualities that theologians refer to as God's **transcendence**. Isaiah's vision of God as high and lifted up, seated upon his heavenly throne, is a vision of his transcendence. Transcendence speaks of God's awesomeness, and immanence speaks of God's presence. These two aspects of God's relationship to us need to be considered carefully when we think about worship. If we overemphasize God's transcendence, we make God too distant and detached from us. A totally transcendent God is out of reach. However, if we overemphasize his immanence, we make God too small and familiar. A totally immanent God is too much like one of us. We worship God because he is awesome and majestic. We also worship God because he is present to save, heal, and deliver us. God is not one of us, but God is among us. God is so great that he cannot be contained, but he makes himself present whenever two or three people come together to worship him.

The three names of the Tabernacle emphasize three different aspects of worship. As the Tent of Meeting, it points to the importance of regular times and places for worship. As the Tabernacle, it points to God's presence in our worship. As the Sanctuary, it points to the majesty and holiness of God.

C. Encountering God in the worship of the Church

The Old Testament tabernacle teaches us about worship, and those lessons are carried over into the New Testament. Jesus declared that the physical building is no longer the center of worship (John 4:21). Instead, the people themselves become the temple in which God dwells. God does not dwell in a temple made with hands. The whole universe is his temple; and, more specifically, the Church is his temple. Therefore, whenever two or three people gather together to worship God, the place becomes the House of God (Matthew 18:20).

1. The Church is the temple of God, a place of worship

As the temple of God, the Church is a place of worship. The Old Testament tabernacle was the dwelling place of God, and the New Testament Church is also the dwelling place of God. As such, the apostle Paul refers to the Church as the "temple of God." He writes, "in whom the whole building, being joined together, grows into a holy **temple** in the LORD, in whom you also are being built together for a **dwelling** place of God in the Spirit" (Ephesians 2:21-22). Writing to the church at Corinth, Paul again uses the terms "temple" and "dwelling" as descriptions of the Church: "Do you not know that you are the **temple** of God and that the Spirit of God **dwells** in you?" (1 Corinthians 3:16). These references to the Church as God's temple suggest that worship is the primary activity of the Church. God's presence in manifested in the Church in a special way. Although we can worship God anywhere, it is in the Church that God has chosen to display his presence and his glory. Because it is the temple of God, the Church is a worshiping community.

In reference to the Church, Paul also uses the phrase "house of God," which is another way of speaking of the temple. He writes to Timothy, "I write so that you may know how you ought to conduct yourself in the **house of God**, which is the **church** of the living God, the pillar and ground of the truth" (1 Timothy 3:15). The understanding of the Church as the house of God is important to the apostle Peter's description of the Church. Peter writes, "Coming to Him as to a living stone, rejected indeed by men, but chosen by God and precious, you also, as living stones, are being built up a **spiritual house**, a holy priesthood, to offer up spiritual sacrifices acceptable to God through Jesus Christ" (1 Peter 2:4-5). Peter emphasizes that the Church serves as a "holy priesthood" that offers "spiritual sacrifices" to the LORD. These spiritual sacrifices consist of the Church's worship.

2. The Church is the family of God, worshiping our Father

As the family of God, the Church worships together. We do not encounter God alone – worship is an activity of the family of God. The apostle Paul writes, "Now, therefore, you are no longer strangers and foreigners, but fellow citizens with the saints and members of the **household** of God" (Ephesians 2:19). The term "household" refers to a family, the family of God. The family of God is also called the "household of faith." Paul says, "Therefore, as we have opportunity, let us do good to all, especially to those who are of the **household** of faith" (Galatians 6:10). Paul clarifies his point by using the word "family" in his letter to the church at Ephesus: "For this reason I bow my knees to the Father of our LORD Jesus Christ, from whom the whole **family** in heaven and earth is named" (Ephesians 3:14-15).

Within this family, God is our Father (Romans 8:15; 1 Peter 1:17; Matthew 6:6-9), and we are the children of God (John 1:12). Members of the Church are like fathers, mothers, sisters, and brothers to us (1 Timothy 5:1-2). As family, we have common parentage, common history, common life together. We worship together as a family, not as a collection of strangers. We worship, serve, fellowship, pray, study, and live in the same household. In the "family," the role of the pastor is to bring the family together in unity, to mediate family squabbles, and to point everyone to the leadership of the Heavenly Father. Family implies commitment. We do not leave our family just because we have a disagreement. Family implies that teaching and discipline must occur within this context of loving commitment.

3. The Church is the fellowship of the saints, worshiping in relationship

As the fellowship of God's people, the Church shares together in worship. The apostle Paul describes the Church as a fellowship. He writes, "God is faithful, by whom you were called into the **fellowship** of His Son, Jesus Christ our LORD" (1 Corinthians 1:9). The word "fellowship" (Greek, *koinonia*) means sharing, caring, and knowing each other. Therefore, worship has a horizontal dimension as well as the vertical dimension. The vertical dimension of worship is our ministry to God in praise and worship. The horizontal dimension is our ministry to the relational needs of one another.

The book of Acts reports both the vertical and horizontal dimensions of worship in the early church. We read:

> And they continued steadfastly in the apostles' doctrine and **fellowship**, in the breaking of bread, and in prayers ... So continuing daily with one accord in the temple, and breaking bread from house to house, they ate their food with gladness and simplicity of heart, **praising God** and having favor with all the people. And the LORD added to the church daily those who were being saved. (Acts 2:42-47)

The early Christians practiced fellowship with one another in their worship; and, at the same time, they praised and glorified God.

What effect does fellowship have on our worship? Leaders must set the example by caring for every person, young and old. Leaders (and the Church as a whole) must love and care for the elderly, the children, and all that are in between. Fellowship is enhanced as we hear each other's stories, testimonies, struggles, and victories (Philippians 2:1). The Church must be structured in a way that intentionally includes times and settings for deep sharing and for mutual prayer, and the pastor must be an example of this sharing and praying for each other.

God created us with the need for relationships. The Garden of Eden was a place of perfection, and everything was "very good" (Genesis 1:31). Nevertheless, when Adam was first created, the LORD said, "It is not good that man should be alone" (Genesis 2:18). Adam was perfect, and his environment was perfect, but Adam was lonely until God created Eve to meet Adam's relational needs.

People today have the same relational needs as Adam. That is why they go to social events, activities, parties, and bars. They need to connect with other people. We learned earlier that the three main goals of worship are to honor God, to strengthen the Church, and to impact the world. The second of these goals involves the connecting of people in relationship. In our times of worship, we encourage one another, we pray for one another, we love one another, we build relationships, and we share what God has done for us. God has called us together to worship in community, in part, to meet the relational needs of his people. We share in the presence and glory of God. We share our burdens, our joys, and our ministry.

D. A passion for the presence of God

1. We desire to encounter God

God's people desire to be in God's presence. On the one hand, we know that God is present everywhere and that he is always with us. On the other hand, there are times when God's presence is manifested in especially powerful ways. We long for those times of encounter with God. The psalmist David expressed his desire to be in God's presence:

> One thing I have desired of the LORD,
>   That will I seek:
> That I may dwell in the house of the LORD
>   All the days of my life,
> To behold the beauty of the LORD,
>   And to inquire in His temple (Psalm 27:4).

The Psalmist prays that he might dwell in the house of the LORD all the days of his life, to "behold the beauty of the LORD, and to inquire in His temple". His statement indicates that the worship of God is his greatest joy. To dwell in the house of the LORD means to remain there at all times. To behold the beauty of the LORD means to see God in all his glory. "Blessed are the pure in heart for they shall see God" (Matthew 5:8).

The deepest desire of God's people is to dwell in the house of the LORD. The same sentiment is found in Psalm 23:6, where David announces, "I will dwell in the house of the LORD forever" and in Psalm 84, where he cries out,

> My soul longs, yes, even faints
>   For the courts of the LORD;
>   My heart and my flesh cry out for the living God …

Blessed are those who dwell in Your house;
They will still be praising You (Psalm 84:2-4).[3]

The one thing that David especially desires is to be in the house of God. It is there among the people of God that David can enjoy the LORD's presence, behold the LORD's beauty, and seek God's face. To be in the house of God is his constant passion; it is the goal and object of his life. Similarly, the early church exhibited a deep desire for constant worship and prayer. Luke reports that the early believers who were newly filled with the spirit continued "with one accord in the temple" (Acts 2:46).

In his role as the King of Israel, David would have faced any number of daily challenges that would have occupied his time. Nevertheless, he chose to make attendance to the house of God one of his highest priorities. David's example should encourage us to evaluate our own priorities. In our technological age we are tempted to relegate the house of God to an afterthought while we are busy pursuing entertainment, pleasure, and affluence.

2. We hunger and thirst for God

History teaches us that a passion for the house of God is a characteristic of revival and spiritual vitality. When God's people are spiritually alert, they do not become weary of assembling together to worship the LORD. But when believers consider it a burden to attend to the services of worship, it is a clear sign of backsliding. David further expresses his passionate desire for the presence of God in Psalm 63:

O God, You are my God;
Early will I seek You;
My soul thirsts for You;
My flesh longs for You In a dry and thirsty land
Where there is no water.
So I have looked for You in the sanctuary,
To see Your power and Your glory (Psalm 63:1-2).

---

[3] See also Psalms 5:8; 23:6; 26:8; 36:9; 42:5; 52:10; 55:15, 65:5; 66:13; 84:11; etc.

To express his passion for God, David uses the language of hunger and thirst. His soul is thirsty for God and his flesh longs for God. The psalmist longs, body and soul, for his God. He longs deeply and passionately for God's presence, a presence that he has experienced in the past. In times of worship, David has encountered God's glory and experienced God's powerful presence.

The Psalmist's 'hunger' and 'thirst' for God is consistent with Pentecostal spirituality, and his desire to encounter God in the sanctuary is consistent with the goals of Pentecostal worship. Pentecostal theologian Chris Green insists that "Pentecostal spirituality is nothing if not a *personal* engagement" with God,[4] a holy desire for God Himself. Like the Psalmist, the Pentecostal community is hungry and thirsty for God and seeks to behold God's power and glory, to lift up their hands in adoration, to testify of past blessings, to praise God with joyful lips, to shout for joy, to stick close to God, to rejoice in God, and to live in hope of the coming reign of God.

3. Worship is the key to encountering God

We are always tempted to replace worship with some other substitute. Some people are the **doers**. Like Martha, they are "distracted with much serving" (Luke 10:40). They think of Christianity as something that we do. They think that it consists in the actions of serving, giving of offerings, and other rituals. Duties and activities are important, but no amount of works can replace worship.

There are others that I would call the **thinkers**. They believe that the heart of Christianity is located in the mind. To them, Christianity is a list of ideas, theological doctrines, and teachings. This kind of people see the sermon as the center of the worship service. They do not enjoy the singing and the worship. They are quick to criticize emotionalism. They want to learn, but no amount of learning can replace worship.

---

[4] Chris E.W. Green, *Toward a Pentecostal Theology of the LORD's Supper: Foretasting the Kingdom* (Cleveland, TN: CPT Press, 2012), p. 289 (emphasis original).

A third group are the **mystics**. Mystics believe that religion is just in your heart, and it involves only our feelings and our emotions. To those people, it does not matter what we believe, and we should not get distracted with deeds of service. To the mystics, everything centers around the feelings of the heart. The doers, the thinkers, and the mystics make the mistake of overemphasizing one aspect of our relationship with God. However, true worship involves loving God with our hearts, our minds, and our actions.

Psalm 63 emphasizes that David's whole person was longing for God. David was a man who loved God and who was hungry and thirsty for God. David had been out in the wilderness, and he knew what it was to be without food and water. He knew how the body begins to develop a thirst and how the body craves water until that thirst is quenched. This is the kind of hunger and thirst that we need today for God.

4. Worship involves seeking God

If we expect to encounter the presence of God, we must follow David's example. First, we must seek God. David said, "O God, You are my God; Early will I seek You" (Psalm 63:1). When David said that he would "seek" God, he means that worship is a necessity – seeking God is a priority. Seeking God is not a luxury or an option. It is our priority.

Second, if we expect to encounter God, we must desire God's power and glory as we have seen him in the sanctuary. Pentecostals believe in the manifestation of God's power – healings, miracles, spiritual gifts, tongues, and prophecy. If we are to see God's power, to experience God's glory, we must have a desire from our heart, and we must pray and ask as Moses prayed, O LORD, "show me Your glory" (Exodus 33:18).

Third, if we want to encounter God, we must expect to be filled. David believed that God would meet his need. He confessed, "my soul shall be satisfied" (Psalm 63:5). David believed that if he sought God, he would be filled. Other scriptures assure us that God "satisfies the longing soul, and fills the hungry soul with goodness" (Psalm 107:9). Jesus gave us the following promise: "blessed are those who hunger and thirst for righteousness, for they shall be filled" (Matthew 5:6). We must expect God to fill us.

5. Pentecostals have a passion for God's presence

The longing for God's presence is described repeatedly in early Pentecostal literature. For example, Alice Flower writes, "All I seemed to sense was a deep craving for the overflowing of His love in my heart. At that moment it seemed I wanted Jesus more than anything in all the world."[5] Reflecting on her passion for God, Zelma E. Argue recalls, "my whole heart seemed to be just one big vacuum craving and crying for God."[6] The rapid growth of the Pentecostal movement is due, in part, to this passion for God's presence. People everywhere have within them a hunger for God, and Pentecostal worship ministers to that hunger.

As Pentecostals, we expect that God will transform our lives during the worship service. God is alive and active, and he will come down in our midst. From Azusa Street until now, Pentecostals everywhere have insisted upon the present reality of God's presence to save, sanctify, fill with the Holy Spirit, heal, and reign as coming king. We expect that God will move in our worship services. Pentecostal theologian Keith Warrington writes, "Two pertinent words when referring to Pentecostal spirituality are 'expectancy' and 'encounter'. Pentecostals expect to encounter God."[7] We expect to see people saved, delivered, and healed. We expect that God will be in the midst of our worship.

---

[5] Alice Reynolds Flower, "My Pentecost," *Assemblies of God Heritage* 20 (Winter 1997-98): 17-20; excerpted from her *Grace for Grace: Some Highlights of God's Grace in the Daily Life of the Flower Family* (Springfield, MO: privately published, 1961).

[6] Cited by Edith Waldvogel Blumhofer, *"Pentecost in My Soul": Explorations in the Meaning of Pentecostal Experience in the Assemblies of God* (Springfield, MO: Gospel Pub. House, 1989), 159.

[7] Keith Warrington, *Pentecostal Theology: A Theology of Encounter* (New York: T & T Clark, 2008), 219. Cf. Daniel E. Albrecht, *Rites in the Spirit: A Ritual Approach to Pentecostal/Charismatic Spirituality* (JPTSup, 17; Sheffield, UK: Sheffield Academic Press, 1999), 226, 38-39.

Conclusion

In this chapter we have learned that worship involves a two-way relationship with God. Not only do we offer our worship to God, but God also offers himself to us in return. We demonstrate our love for God through our worship, and God demonstrates his love for us through the manifestation of his presence in our midst. Therefore, worship is a deep and powerful encounter between God and God's people.

Questions for Review and Application

1. List three biblical examples of people who encountered the presence of God in worship.

2. Share three reasons why worship is necessary.

3. What were Israel's three major feasts, and what did they signify?

4. Explain how the covenant undergirds corporate worship.

5. List the three primary names for the tabernacle along with their definitions.

6. Define the term immanence.

7. Define the term transcendence.

8. Read John 4:21 and Matthew 18:20. What do they teach about the place or location of worship?

9. List three scriptures that speak of the Church as God's temple.

10. How is our worship impacted by the fact that the Church is a family?

11. List three ways that worship fulfills the relational needs of believers.

12. Write Psalm 27:4.

13. Explain David's symbolic language of hunger and thirst. How does it relate to worship?

14. List and define the three types of people who overemphasize one aspect of their relationship with God.

15. Name the three ways that we must follow David's example if we expect to encounter God.

16. Share how Pentecostals express their passion for God's presence.

17. In our times of worship, how does God express his love for us?

CHAPTER 5

WORSHIP IN THE BEAUTY OF HOLINESS

Give unto the LORD the glory due to His name; Worship the LORD in the beauty of holiness (Psalm 29:2).

A. The beauty of holiness

1. The example of King David

When David became king of Israel, he brought the tabernacle into Jerusalem and made Jerusalem the center of worship. Inside the tabernacle was the Ark of the Covenant, which represented the throne of God and the presence of God. We observed in Chapter 3 that as David led the procession that carried the Ark of the Covenant, he "danced before the LORD with all his might," and he was clothed with only a linen garment (2 Samuel 6:12-15). As the king of Israel, David was authorized to wear his royal garments at all times. However, David chose to lay aside his beautiful robes as he worshiped the LORD. David was adorned only with the holiness of God, not with human beauty. He worshiped the LORD "in the beauty of holiness" (Psalm 29:2).

2. The example of the priests

Similarly, the priests of Israel wore beautiful robes when they were in the presence of the people, but they removed those robes when they entered the Holy of Holies. Therefore, the adornment of the priests was to display to the people the beauty of God (Exodus 28:2-40). Their adornment was a sign to the people, representing the glory of God. However, when they came into the presence of God, the priests wore only pure white robes (Leviticus 16:4). God did not desire to see the beauty of physical ornamentation, rather he wanted to see the beauty of holiness, as symbolized by the white robes.

3. Who may worship God?

To worship God in the beauty of holiness means that we come to God in humility. We realize that we are not worthy to enter into God's presence. We do not approach God on the basis of our reputation, our works, our accomplishments, our attire, our knowledge, or our name. We approach God through the blood of Jesus alone (Hebrews 4:15-16). The psalmist explained that if we want to worship in the beauty of holiness, we must be holy. He wrote,

> Who may ascend into the hill of the LORD?
>   Or who may stand in His holy place?
> He who has clean hands and a pure heart,
>   Who has not lifted up his soul to an idol,
>   Nor sworn deceitfully.
> He shall receive blessing from the LORD,
>   And righteousness from the God of his salvation.
> (Psalm 24:3-5)

To worship the LORD in the beauty of holiness means that we enter into worship with a pure heart. Jesus said, "Blessed are the pure in heart, for they shall see God" (Matthew 5:8). If our hearts are impure, then we must purify them. James wrote that when we draw near to God we should "cleanse" our hands and "purify" our hearts (James 4:8). The writer of Hebrews adds the following instruction: "let us draw near with a true heart in full assurance of faith, having our hearts sprinkled from an evil conscience and our bodies washed with pure water" (Hebrews 10:22). The apostle Paul agreed that God desires a holy people to worship him. Paul writes, "let us cleanse ourselves from all filthiness of the flesh and spirit, perfecting holiness in the fear of God" (2 Corinthians 7:1).

B. Worshiping on holy ground

1. The example of Moses

We must worship God in the beauty of holiness because the place where we encounter God is holy ground. For example, Moses met

God on the backside of the desert. There was nothing unusual or special about the soil at that location. However, when he appeared to Moses, God said, "Take your sandals off your feet, for the place where you stand is holy ground" (Exodus 3:5). The ground became holy because God was present.

2. The teaching of Jesus

Jesus taught us that where any two or three are gathered together, he is in the midst of them. The presence of Jesus makes the ground holy. It is a holy place to God, and we should treat it that way. Wherever we worship, we should treat it as a place of worship, a place of reverence, a holy place. God's presence sanctifies the place and makes it holy. God is holy, but God is also present with us. To be able to encounter the holy God is a vital part of worship. We come together to encounter this holy God.

C. Worship requires reverence toward God

To worship God in the beauty of holiness means that we show proper reverence to the House of God. The LORD gave detailed instructions to Israel concerning the building of the tabernacle, the offering of sacrifices, and the work of the priests. The first high priest was Aaron, and the first priests were Aaron's sons Nadab and Abihu. These men were anointed and consecrated to the office of the priesthood.

Sadly, the sons of Aaron made a mess of things very quickly by ignoring the explicit instructions that the LORD had given for worship:

> Then Nadab and Abihu, the sons of Aaron, each took his censer and put fire in it, put incense on it, and offered profane fire before the LORD, which He had not commanded them. So fire went out from the LORD and devoured them, and they died before the LORD (Leviticus 10:1-2).

The pillar of fire that had gone before Israel in the wilderness and protected them every night was now turned against these two men. It was the same fire of God that had come down from heaven and consumed the sacrifice on the day that Nadab and Abihu were consecrated as priests. Their illicit worship was an abomination to God, and God responded with severe judgment. God's judgment upon these two brothers should remind us that our worship is taken very seriously by God. God desires that we worship him in the beauty of holiness.

The sin of these two men was in offering "profane fire before the LORD, which He had not commanded them" (Leviticus 10:1). This sin involves four elements.

1. Entering the Holy of Holies without authorization
The LORD had made it clear that only the high priest could enter into the Holy of Holies and that even he could enter only at certain times of the year. Even Aaron would die if he entered at the wrong time:

> Now the LORD spoke to Moses after the death of the two sons of Aaron, when they offered profane fire before the LORD, and died; and the LORD said to Moses: "Tell Aaron your brother not to come at just any time into the Holy Place inside the veil, before the mercy seat which is on the ark, lest he die; for I will appear in the cloud above the mercy seat" (Leviticus 16:1-2).

Clearly, these two brothers approached the presence of the LORD uninvited and unauthorized. They presumed for themselves the authority to enter in to the most holy place before the Ark of the Covenant, which violated God's specific commands. In so doing, they placed themselves above the position of the high priest and above the commands of God. Their worship was according to their own initiative. They worshiped God in a way that was not authorized.

2. Showing a lack of reverence
The attitude of Nadab and Abihu was a failure to show reverence for God and his sanctuary. The worship of God is a holy activity, and God expects those who worship him to do so with great reverence and fear: "And Moses said to Aaron, 'This is what the LORD spoke, saying: "By those who come near Me I must be regarded as holy; And before all the people I must be glorified."' So Aaron held his peace" (Leviticus 10:3). Nadab and Abihu had not shown

reverence for the LORD, and the LORD would not tolerate this irreverence from these men who had been so greatly blessed and who were in a position of leadership in Israel.

3. Offering profane fire

They offered to God something profane, which means something that was not sanctified, something that was not holy. The profane fire was burning coals taken from a source other than the one specified by God. Only the fire from God's altar was to be allowed in the holy place (Leviticus 16:12-13).

God had given to them detailed instructions as to exactly what he required of them. The incense burners that they used when they entered into the holy place belonged as part of the equipment of the temple, and they were as sacred as the altar itself. Because the incense burners were holy, the only fire that was allowed in those burners must also be holy, that is, fire that came from the holy altar. These two priests should have known that what they were doing was wrong, but apparently they had no fear of God. The LORD had specified that only coals of fire from the altar should be burned in these incense burners. However, these two men worshiped as they saw fit rather than worshiping according to God's commandment.

4. Worshiping while intoxicated

We are inclined to wonder why these men would so clearly disobey God. They were not ignorant of God's will. They knew that they were not authorized to enter the Holy of Holies. They knew also that only coals from the altar were to be placed in the incense burner. Apparently, their judgment was hindered by the fact that they were drunk. As soon as their bodies had been dragged outside the camp, the LORD said to their father Aaron,

> Do not drink wine or intoxicating drink, you, nor your sons with you, when you go into the tabernacle of meeting, lest you die. It shall be a statute forever throughout your generations, that you may distinguish between holy and unholy, and between unclean and clean (Leviticus 10:9-10).

Because Nadab and Abihu had indulged in some kind of wine or strong drink, they were incapacitated for distinguishing between the holy fire and its unholy counterfeit. Even though they knew the difference, drunkenness had rendered them unable to make the proper distinction. Their senses were dulled and their judgment was impaired.

We should not forget God's judgment upon these two men. This story is in the Bible for a reason, and that reason is that we might learn from it. Apparently, King Uzziah had forgotten the story of Nadab and Abihu. He entered the temple to burn incense to the LORD, but burning the incense was the ministry of the priest only. The King was not allowed in the holy place. Because of his violation of God's holiness, Uzziah was turned into a leper (2 Chronicles 26:18-21). We must worship God according to the directions that God has given us, and we must not depart from the LORD's Commandments in worship. To worship any other way will cause God to become very angry. These stories remind us that when we present ourselves before God, we must come to him in holy reverence.

D. Worship requires righteousness toward our neighbor

1. Loving God and loving one's neighbor

To worship the LORD in the beauty of holiness means that we show reverence toward God and toward his house. It also means that we behave rightly toward our neighbor. The great commandment states, "You shall love the LORD your God with all your heart, with all your soul, and with all your mind," and the second greatest commandment is "You shall love your neighbor as yourself" (Matthew 22:37-39). Worship is one way that we demonstrate and express our love for God. However, we sometimes overlook the fact that the two great commandments are linked together. We must give serious consideration to the following warning:

> If someone says, "I love God," and hates his brother, he is a liar; for he who does not love his brother whom he has seen, how can he love God whom he has not seen? And this commandment we have from Him: that he who loves God must love his brother also (1 John 4:20-21).

Therefore, to worship God in the beauty of holiness also means that we must show love toward our neighbor. If we do not love our neighbor, then our worship is not accepted by God.

Because worship is an activity of the believing community, any offense against one's neighbor is also a breach of worship. Our beliefs, our worship, and our ethics are deeply interconnected. How we pray and worship is linked to how we live and to how we behave toward others. We cannot separate our worship from our manner of life because everything that we are and everything that we have belongs to God.

2. Worship is deeply connected to ethics

Unfortunately, we have overlooked the fact that worship is directly connected to our ethics. Many years ago, Christians would worship God; but, at the same time, they would buy and sell as slaves people made in the image of God. Even now, some people worship on Sunday and abuse their children or spouses on Monday. Christian business people sometimes disconnect their faith from their unjust business practices.

Worship connects to ethics because worship flows out of the covenant relationship between God and his people. The people of God should be a new kind of community, a community of love, justice, acceptance, and care. The Old Testament prophets call upon Israel to be a righteous people who do not oppress one another. Likewise, the book of Psalms praises the righteous and condemns the wicked, because "the LORD knows the way of the righteous, but the way of the wicked will perish" (Psalm 1:6). The righteous are like a 'tree planted by the rivers of water' (Psalm 1:3) and they "flourish like the palm tree and grow like a cedar" (Psalm 92:12). The LORD hears the "cry" of the righteous, but his face is "against those who do evil" (Psalm 34:15-16).

3. God wants righteousness in his worshipers

When we think of righteousness, we tend to describe it as a right relationship to God. However, the biblical view of righteousness includes right relationships with other people around us. Righteousness is more than an abstract quality – it produces ethical actions. The righteous are generous, lending to their neighbors, and they give "freely" to "the poor" (Psalm 112:5-9). Moreover, the righteous "turn away from evil" (Psalm 37:27). The wicked person, however, "plots destruction" and loves "evil more than good" (Psalm 52:1-5). Therefore, because "Yahweh loves justice, he will not forsake his saints ... but the children of the wicked shall be cut off" (Psalm 37:26-28). The Psalmist says to the wicked, "God will break you down forever; he will snatch and tear you from your tent; he will uproot you from the land of the living" (Psalm 52:4-5).

Righteousness and justice are attributes of God, – "He loves righteousness and justice" (Psalm 33:4-5) – and those attributes are also demanded in society. Israel is commanded, "Give justice to the weak and the fatherless; maintain the right of the afflicted and the destitute. Rescue the weak and the needy; deliver them from the hand of the wicked" (Psalm 82:1-4). Along with the command comes a promise: "Blessed is the one who considers the poor! In the day of trouble the LORD delivers him" (Psalm 41.1). During worship, we learn what kind of people we ought to be. In worship, we learn to minister to the needs of others, and we make a commitment to serve others.

4. The ethical requirements of worship

a. Psalm 15

Worship is an expression of relationship. Therefore, worship cannot be separated from the Bible's demand for justice within the community. Therefore, the genuineness or validity of our worship is judged, in part, by how we treat our neighbor. God accepts only worship that is offered by a just and righteous congregation. Psalm 15 sets forth the ethical requirements for acceptable worship:

> LORD, who may abide in Your tabernacle?
> 　Who may dwell in Your holy hill?
> He who walks uprightly,
> 　And works righteousness,
> 　And speaks the truth in his heart;
> He who does not backbite with his tongue,
> 　Nor does evil to his neighbor,
> 　Nor does he take up a reproach against his friend; ...

He who does not put out his money at usury,
　　Nor does he take a bribe against the innocent.
　　He who does these things shall never be moved (Psalm
15:1-5. See also Psalms 5.3-7; 24.2-4; 50.15-20; 101.3-7).

Psalm 15 establishes the relationship between worship and conduct. It highlights important characteristics of the true worshiper. Many of these qualities are related directly to how the worshiper treats their neighbor. The mention of the "tabernacle" establishes the setting of this Psalm to be worship. Whose worship is acceptable to God? A true worshiper has integrity, does what is right, and speaks truthfully. A true worshiper does not slander, or do evil, or listen to gossip. A true worshiper does not demand interest on a loan or take a bribe against the innocent. Each of these characteristics relates to the command to love one's neighbor. If we do not behave in these positive ways toward our neighbor, God does not accept our worship.

b. The prophet Isaiah

The prophet Isaiah states even more clearly the LORD's refusal to accept worship from those who do not love their neighbor. He insists that pious acts of worship do not please God if our lives are not holy. Isaiah declares,

Bring no more futile sacrifices;
　　Incense is an abomination to Me.
The New Moons, the Sabbaths, and the calling of assemblies –
　　I cannot endure iniquity and the sacred meeting.
Your New Moons and your appointed feasts My soul hates;
　　They are a trouble to Me, I am weary of bearing them.
When you spread out your hands,
　　I will hide My eyes from you;
Even though you make many prayers,
　　I will not hear. Your hands are full of blood.
Wash yourselves, make yourselves clean;
　　Put away the evil of your doings from before My eyes.
　　Cease to do evil,
Learn to do good;
　　Seek justice,
　　Rebuke the oppressor;

Defend the fatherless,
Plead for the widow (Isaiah 1:13-17).

Isaiah mentions many important elements of Old Testament worship: sacrifices, incense, holy days, sacred feasts, and prayer. However, all of these rituals of worship are an "abomination" to God, and he "hates" them. He is "weary of bearing them." He refuses to hear their prayers, and he will "hide" his eyes from looking upon them. God's refusal to accept Israel's worship is tied directly to their abuse of their neighbor. If they want God to receive their worship, they must "seek justice, rebuke the oppressor, defend the orphan, and plead for the widow." In other words, they must love their neighbor, especially their weak and helpless neighbor.

c. The prophet Amos

The prophet Amos declares a similar judgment against Israel. He insists that acts of worship are not a substitute for acts of justice. The LORD says,

I hate, I despise your feast days,
And I do not savor your sacred assemblies.
Though you offer Me burnt offerings and your grain offerings,
I will not accept them,
Nor will I regard your fattened peace offerings.
Take away from Me the noise of your songs,
For I will not hear the melody of your stringed instruments.
But let justice run down like water,
And righteousness like a mighty stream (Amos 5:21-24).

Clearly, Israel's worship was not acceptable to God because they had forsaken "justice" and "righteousness." These two qualities are directly related to how we treat our neighbor.

d. The New Testament

The connection between worship and ethics is carried over into the New Testament as well. In the Gospel of Matthew, we read that Jesus was concerned about the purity of the temple:

Then Jesus went into the temple of God and drove out all those who bought and sold in the temple, and overturned the tables of the money changers and the seats of those who sold doves. And He said to them, "It is written, 'My house shall be called a house of prayer,' but you have made it a 'den of thieves'" (Matthew 21:12-13).

Jesus drove out the merchants because, in those days, the money changers were corrupt, and those who sold doves would raise the price to make excessive profit. They were taking advantage of the poor and were robbing them. Jesus described them as a "den of thieves."

When the apostle Paul is giving instructions about the LORD's Supper, he rebukes those who were mistreating the brothers and sisters who were poor. He accused the wealthy of shaming "those who have nothing" (1 Corinthians 11:22). Because of their unethical behavior in the house of God, these abusers had been judged by God. Many of them had become sick, and some had even died.

Poor people are not treated very well in some churches. We read in the Epistle of James that some churches were showing partiality to the rich, and in so doing "have dishonored the poor man" (James 2:6). He points out that when people enter the church to worship, they all should be treated with respect. James writes further,

If you really fulfill the royal law according to the Scripture, "You shall love your neighbor as yourself," you do well; but if you show partiality, you commit sin, and are convicted by the law as transgressors (James 2:8-9).

According to James, the LORD is looking for a people who will worship God while showing love and respect for everyone. This is worshiping God in the beauty of holiness. As the apostle Paul stated, worshipers should be holy. We should lift up "holy hands" unto God in worship (1 Timothy 2:8).

Conclusion

We are invited to worship the LORD in the beauty of holiness. When God looks upon our worship, he does not judge us according to our talent, our resources, or our sophistication. He judges our worship by our holiness. Do we love God and love our neighbor? If so, then our worship is a sweet aroma unto the LORD.

Questions for Review and Application

1. In what way is David an example of worshiping the Lord in the beauty of holiness?

2. What did the beauty of the priestly garments represent?

3. Name three characteristics of a genuine worshiper as found in Psalms 24.

4. Give three New Testament scriptures that tell us to be holy in our worship.

5. What made the ground holy in Exodus 3:5?

6. What is it that makes the house of God holy today?

7. Who were the first priests in Israel?

8. Nadab and Abihu were judged for false worship. Explain the four elements of their sin.

   (1)

   (2)

   (3)

   (4)

9. What was King Uzziah's punishment for entering the Holy Place without God's approval?

10. What are the two greatest commandments?

11. According to 1 John 4:20-21, what is the relationship between loving God and loving one's neighbor?

12. Explain the connection between belief, worship, and ethics.

13. What happens when we overlook the connection between worship and ethics?

14. How are the righteous and the wicked contrasted in the Psalms?

15. What are the characteristics of the righteous?

16. How is our righteousness expressed toward those in need?

17. List the attributes of a genuine worshiper according to Psalm 15.

18. According to Isaiah 1, what elements of our worship are important to God?

19. According to the prophet Amos, why would God refuse to accept Israel's worship?

20. Why did Jesus describe the temple as a "den of thieves"?

21. Why were people getting sick in Corinth during the Lord's Supper?

22. How does James explain the command to love one's neighbor in relation to worship?

~∞⌒ CHAPTER 6 ⌒∞~

WORSHIP IN SPIRIT AND IN TRUTH

God is Spirit, and those who worship Him must worship in spirit and truth (John 4:24).

A. Spirit and Truth

1. The fuel of worship

It should be clear by now that the Bible has much to say about worship. We have studied the importance of worship, the definition of worship, and the purpose of worship. We have discussed worship as an encounter with God, and we have explained what it means to worship in the beauty of holiness. Every topic that we have studied is vitally important; however, we have yet to discover the most important lesson regarding worship, which is: **true worship is empowered by the Holy Spirit**. Without the Holy Spirit, true worship is impossible to attain. True worship is initiated by the Holy Spirit, guided by the Holy Spirit, and inspired by the Holy Spirit.

When a beautiful new car rolls off of the assembly line, it has everything it needs. It has wheels, tires, seats, and doors. The paint is shiny and new. The engine is in perfect condition. In order to race across the country, it needs only one more thing. It requires gasoline. Without gasoline, the engine will not run, and the wheels will not turn. Without gasoline, a new car is just an expensive curiosity, in which we could sit and listen to the radio. As gasoline is the fuel for an automobile, the Holy Spirit is the fuel of worship.

2. True worshipers

a. The woman at the well

The key New Testament text for understanding the value of the Holy Spirit in worship is John 4:18-26, where we read about Jesus' encounter with the Samaritan woman at Jacob's Well. Jesus was traveling north from Judea to Galilee, and he passed through the Samaritan city of Sychar. The Jews normally tried to avoid Samaria because of the longstanding hostilities between the Jews and the Samaritans. However, Jesus had a mission to fulfill; so he paused at Jacob's Well, where he met a Samaritan woman who had come to draw water.

The woman was quite surprised when Jesus asked her for a drink of water, because the Jews had no dealings with the Samaritans. Jesus and the woman carried on a conversation about "living water" and "eternal life," and then Jesus revealed his knowledge of her personal life. At that point, the woman perceived that Jesus was a prophet:

> The woman said to Him, "Sir, I perceive that You are a prophet. Our fathers worshiped on this mountain, and you Jews say that in Jerusalem is the place where one ought to worship." Jesus said to her, "Woman, believe Me, the hour is coming when you will neither on this mountain, nor in Jerusalem, worship the Father. You worship what you do not know; we know what we worship, for salvation is of the Jews. But the hour is coming, and now is, when the true worshipers will worship the Father in spirit and truth; for the Father is seeking such to worship Him. God is Spirit, and those who worship Him must **worship in spirit and truth**." The woman said to Him, "I know that Messiah is coming" (who is called Christ). "When He comes, He will tell us all things." Jesus said to her, "I who speak to you am He" (John 4:18-26).

b. The location of worship

The conversation about worship teaches us several valuable lessons. First, regarding the place of worship, Jesus points out that the day is coming when worshipers will gather anywhere and everywhere to worship God. The New Covenant and the outpouring of the Holy Spirit will make worship a universal experience. Location will no longer be important, because God will dwell in the hearts of his people and in the midst of the Church, wherever it is located.

c. The object of worship

Second, regarding the object of worship, Jesus declares that the Samaritans did not know who they worshiped. The Jews, however, knew who they worshiped, because salvation comes through the Jews. The Samaritans had only a partial faith, because they accepted only the Old Testament books of Genesis through Deuteronomy as Scripture. By excluding most of the Old Testament, they had failed to adopt much of the biblical faith. The Samaritans represent anyone who believes only part of the Bible, but they do not accept the whole Bible. That kind of faith is incomplete and imperfect.

According to Jesus, the object of true worship is "the Father." We discussed the object of worship in Chapter 3, so it is not necessary to repeat it here. As a reminder, however, we might state only that Christians worship Jehovah, the God of the Bible. There is no other God (Isaiah 45:21). We worship Jehovah because he is creator of all things, he is our only savior, and he is our covenant God. To worship "in truth" means that we do not worship other gods; we do not worship created things; we do not worship angels; we do not worship demons; and we do not worship other humans.

When we say that we worship only Jehovah, we are including the entire Trinity – Father, Son, and Holy Spirit. The first chapter of John's Gospel reveals that Jesus is God (John 1:1). All things were created by the Father through Jesus (John 1:3). To worship "in truth" means that we worship Jesus as our Savior, Sanctifier, Spirit Baptizer, Healer, and soon coming King.

It is important for pastors and worship leaders to remember that worship not only inspires, but it also teaches. Most Christians learn their theology in the Sunday worship services. Our beliefs about God are expressed in our worship. We learn about God through the songs, the prayers, the testimonies, and the sermons. Our worship embodies our theology, celebrates our theology, and communicates our theology. Therefore, we must conduct our worship services so that they teach sound doctrine. When evaluating our worship, we should ask what kind of theology our worship conveys.

d. The nature of worship

Third, regarding the nature of worship, Jesus taught that "true worshipers will worship the Father in spirit and truth." In John's Gospel, Jesus is the truth. He is "full of grace and truth" (John 1:15, 17). Jesus speaks the truth and testifies to the truth (John 8:40, 45, 46; 18:37). In fact, Jesus Christ **is the truth**. He is "the way, the truth, and the life" (John 14:6). Therefore, those who worship in truth are worshiping the Father in the Spirit and in the Truth (Jesus). Jesus' statement hints at the fact that true worship involves the entire trinity: Father, Son, and Holy Spirit.

To worship God in spirit and truth is necessary because God is spirit. Earlier in the Gospel of John, we learned that to become children of God we must be "born of the Spirit" (John 3:5-6). Now we discover that the Spirit is necessary not only for the new birth but also for true worship.[1] We are born by the Spirit, and we also worship in the Spirit.

e. Power for worship

The Holy Spirit is the power of worship that enables us to connect with God. The apostle Paul recognizes the importance of the Spirit in worship. He writes, "For we are the circumcision, who **worship God in the Spirit**, rejoice in Christ Jesus, and have no confidence in the flesh" (Philippians 3:3). Without the Holy Spirit, we do not have the ability to worship God acceptably or freely. The human flesh is weak and incapable of worship. Only "in the Spirit" can we truly worship God.

According to Paul, being filled with the Spirit leads naturally to joyful worship. Worship in the Spirit includes "singing" and "giving thanks". Paul writes,

> And do not be drunk with wine, in which is dissipation; but be filled with the **Spirit**, speaking to one another in psalms and hymns and spiritual songs, singing and making melody in your

---

[1] See John Christopher Thomas, *The Spirit of the New Testament* (Blandford Forum, UK: Deo Publishing, 2005), p. 161-62.

heart to the LORD, giving thanks always for all things to God the Father in the name of our LORD Jesus Christ" (Ephesians 5:18-20).

f. The Spirit of truth

We tend to separate the two terms – "spirit" and "truth" – but Jesus makes the point that genuine worship requires a merging of both. We know that Jesus is the truth, but the Spirit is also the truth. The Spirit and the truth are intimately connected. Later in the Gospel of John, Jesus will teach his disciples that the Holy Spirit is the "Spirit of truth." Jesus says, "And I will pray the Father, and He will give you another Helper, that He may abide with you forever – the Spirit of truth, whom the world cannot receive" (John 14:16-17; 15:26). Furthermore, as the Spirit of truth, the Spirit will guide us into the truth and teach us all things: "when He, the Spirit of truth, has come, He will guide you into all truth" (John 16:13). "But the Helper, the Holy Spirit, whom the Father will send in My name, He will teach you all things" (John 14:26).

B. In the Spirit

To worship God in the Spirit includes several related elements. In the New Testament, Spirit inspired worship is characterized by rejoicing in the Spirit, praying in the Spirit, and being in the Spirit on the LORD's Day.

1. Rejoicing in the Spirit

The Holy Spirit produces joy. The apostle Paul tells us that joy is a fruit of the Spirit. He states, "But the fruit of the **Spirit** is love, **joy**, peace, longsuffering, kindness, goodness, faithfulness, gentleness, self-control" (Galatians 5:22-23). In fact, joy is so important that it is a characteristic of the kingdom: "for the kingdom of God is not eating and drinking, but righteousness and peace and **joy in the Holy Spirit**" (Romans 14:17). Like the first Christians, we are born of the Spirit, and we should be filled with the Spirit. Those first Christians experienced the joy of the Holy Spirit: "And the disciples were filled with joy and with the Holy Spirit" (Acts 13:52). Of course, Jesus Christ is our greatest example, and he also worshiped the Father in the Spirit. When the seventy disciples returned from their mission trip, Jesus worshiped the LORD: "In that hour Jesus **rejoiced in the Spirit**" (Luke 10:21). Like the early Christians and like Jesus himself, we should worship with joy in the Holy Spirit.

2. Praying in the Spirit

Prayer is an act of worship, and every worship service includes prayer. When we pray, we are expressing our needs and desires to God. However, we must have the Spirit's help in order to make our prayers honest and effective. Paul explains: "Likewise the **Spirit** also helps in our weaknesses. For we do not know what we should **pray** for as we ought, but the Spirit Himself makes intercession for us with groanings which cannot be uttered" (Romans 8:26). We may not know what we really need or how to ask in the proper manner, but the Holy Spirit directs, empowers, and energizes our prayers. We must pray "in the Spirit." Paul states that the Spirit prays for us with "groanings that cannot be uttered." These groanings refer to praying in tongues, as Paul reveals in another text, where he writes, "For if I **pray in a tongue**, my spirit prays, but my understanding is unfruitful. What is the conclusion then? I will **pray with the spirit**, and I will also pray with the understanding. I will sing with the spirit, and I will also sing with the understanding" (1 Corinthians 14:14-15).

Both Paul and Jude emphasize the necessity of praying in the Spirit. Paul encourages to be "praying always with all prayer and supplication **in the Spirit**" (Ephesians 6:18). Jude adds that when we pray "in the Spirit" we are building our faith: "But you, beloved, building yourselves up on your most holy faith, **praying in the Holy Spirit**" (Jude 1:20). Worship in the Spirit includes praying in the Spirit.

3. In the Spirit on the LORD's Day

The prophet Joel predicted that in the last days God would pour out his Spirit upon all flesh. As a result of this outpouring, believers would experience prophecy, dreams, visions, signs, and wonders (Joel 2:28-32). Joel's prophecy was fulfilled on the Day of Pentecost, when the Holy Spirit filled Jesus' disciples. They spoke in tongues and proclaimed the "wonderful works of God" (Acts

2:1-11). After being filled with the Spirit, the early Christians experienced "signs and wonders" (Acts 2:19, 22, 43; 5:12; 6:8; 7:36; 8:13; 14:3; Romans 15:19; Hebrews 2:4).

Many of these experiences happened as the believers worshiped the LORD together every Sunday, which was called the LORD's Day. John was exiled on the Isle of Patmos for preaching the gospel, but he continued to worship God. Joel's prophecy was fulfilled in John's life as he worshiped in the Spirit. John writes, "I was **in the Spirit** on the LORD's Day, and I heard behind me a loud voice, as of a trumpet" (Revelation 1:10). The entire book of Revelation is a record of John's visions in the Spirit.

It is not unusual for Pentecostal worshipers to have experiences similar to those of John. Many Pentecostals have testified to signs, wonders, and visions that came to them during a worship service. At times, Pentecostal worshipers have fallen to the floor as they were carried by the Spirit into the presence of God where they saw visions. Some people call this experience being "slain in the Spirit."

Still another example of being "in the Spirit" on the LORD's Day is Pentecostal preaching. The apostle Paul insisted that preaching should be inspired by the Spirit, and it should be accompanied by the works of the Spirit. He wrote,

> And my speech and my preaching were not with persuasive words of human wisdom, but in demonstration of the **Spirit** and of power, that your faith should not be in the wisdom of men but in the power of God (1 Corinthians 2:4-5).

When the preacher is "in the Spirit," the worship service will be more effective. When the preacher is "in the Spirit," the people will experience the presence of God and will be able to say with David, "I rejoice at Your word As one who finds great treasure" (Psalm 119:162).

C. Gifts of the Spirit

1. Worship in the Spirit includes the gifts of the Spirit

If it is necessary that we worship "in spirit and in truth," then all aspects of the Spirit's work must be considered. One way that the Spirit manifests himself in our worship is through the gifts of the Spirit. Paul explains that the spiritual gifts are part of worship in the Spirit. He writes, "For he who speaks in a tongue does not speak to men but to God, for no one understands him; however, **in the spirit** he speaks mysteries" (1 Corinthians 14:2).

2. Gifts of God's grace

In most cases, the term "spiritual gifts" is a translation of the Greek word *charismata*, which is derived from the root word *charis*, meaning **grace**. Therefore, the spiritual gifts might more accurately be called **grace gifts**. Spiritual gifts are a part of salvation – they are God's grace flowing through us. As gifts of God's grace, the spiritual gifts are not hidden talents; they are supernatural endowments from God. The gifts are part of our participation in the work of God, the ministry of God's grace, the church, and salvation. The spiritual gifts are ministry through which we give to one another.

Too often, we desire only to receive, but the gifts are God's work that flows through us to others. Each person has gifts that will meet the needs of other people, and other people have gifts that will meet our needs. Through the spiritual gifts, we minister to each other. The ministry of spiritual gifts assumes that we are meeting together as the Body of Christ in worship.

3. Spiritual gifts according to Peter

There are four major passages in the New Testament that teach us about the spiritual gifts, and we will look briefly at each of them. First, we will consider the comments of Peter:

> As each one has received a **gift**, minister it to one another, as good stewards of the manifold grace of God. If anyone speaks, let him speak as the oracles of God. If anyone ministers, let him do it as with the ability which God supplies, that in all things God may be glorified through Jesus Christ (1 Peter 4:10-11).

Peter's reference to the spiritual gifts emphasizes three important aspects of the gifts: 1. The gifts are a stewardship bestowed upon us. We do not own them, but we are allowed to use them. 2. The gifts should be used in ministry, that is, in service to others. 3. Every gift should be exercised with humility, in the strength and ability that God gives. 4. The gifts should always glorify God. We do not receive the glory.

4. Spiritual gifts in the book of Romans

The three remaining Scripture passages about the spiritual gifts are found in Paul's writings. To the church at Rome, Paul writes,

> For as we have many members in one body, but all the members do not have the same function, so we, being many, are one body in Christ, and individually members of one another. Having then **gifts** differing according to the grace that is given to us, let us use them: if prophecy, let us prophesy in proportion to our faith; or ministry, let us use it in our ministering; he who teaches, in teaching; he who exhorts, in exhortation; he who gives, with liberality; he who leads, with diligence; he who shows mercy, with cheerfulness (Romans 12:4-8).

The gifts that Paul lists here are prophecy, ministry (serving), teaching, exhorting (encouraging), giving, leading, and showing mercy. These gifts not only come to us out of God's grace, but also, they should be exercised in proportion to the grace that God gives to us. We cannot operate these gifts in our own strength. Paul emphasizes here that the Body of Christ has many different members, and each member may have a different gift. Nevertheless, we are still but one body, serving the LORD in unity.

5. Ministry gifts in the book of Ephesians

Paul's reference to gifts in his letter to the Ephesians focuses upon what some people call gifts of ministry. However, the source of the gifts is still the grace of God, the same as the other gifts.

> But to each one of us **grace** was given according to the measure of Christ's gift ... And He Himself gave some to be apostles, some prophets, some evangelists, and some pastors and

teachers, for the equipping of the saints for the work of ministry, for the edifying of the Body of Christ, till we all come to the unity of the faith (Ephesians 4:7-13).

Paul names five ministry gifts: apostle, prophet, evangelist, pastor, and teacher. Some scholars would argue that there are only four gifts, and that pastor and teacher should go together as one role: "pastor-teacher." The purpose of these leadership gifts includes equipping others for service and of discerning the giftedness of the members. As in other Scriptures, the goal of the gifts is that the Body of Christ may be edified and unified.

6. Gifts of the Spirit in the book of 1 Corinthians

a. The spiritual gifts are important

The most extensive discussion of the spiritual gifts is found in Paul's first letter to the church at Corinth, where his discussion of the gifts spans three chapters (12-14). In our study of such a lengthy discussion, we might be tempted to overlook Paul's first comment, but it should not go unnoticed. Paul says, "Now concerning spiritual gifts, brethren, I do not want you to be ignorant" (1 Corinthians 12:1). Apparently, Paul wants us to be aware of the importance of the spiritual gifts. He does not want anyone to be uninformed of their nature, their value, their purpose, and their operation.

b. All the gifts have the same source and goal

Humans often place a greater value on the most visible of the gifts, such as tongues and prophecy. Paul, however, wants us to know that all of the gifts are valuable.

There are diversities of gifts, but the same Spirit. There are differences of ministries, but the same LORD. And there are diversities of activities, but it is the same God who works all in all. But the manifestation of the Spirit is given to each one for the profit of all (1 Corinthians 12:4-7).

Paul emphasizes the threefold working of the gifts in relation to the threefold nature of the Trinity. There are different "gifts," "ministries," and "activities;" and the workings of the gifts are directed by "the same Spirit," "the same LORD," and "the same God." Paul also stresses that point that the gifts are not given for the benefit of only the one person who exercises the gift – the gifts are given "for the profit of all." That is, the gifts may be different, but they all are given to benefit the entire Church.

c. The Spirit gives these gifts

Paul lists the gifts, stating clearly that each gift is given "through the same Spirit." He states:

> for to one is given the word of wisdom through the Spirit, to another the word of knowledge through the same Spirit, to another faith by the same Spirit, to another gifts of healings by the same Spirit, to another the working of miracles, to another prophecy, to another discerning of spirits, to another different kinds of tongues, to another the interpretation of tongues. But one and the same Spirit works all these things, distributing to each one individually as He wills (1 Corinthians 12:8-11).

Paul names nine spiritual gifts:

1. The word of wisdom. Wisdom is a combination of superior skill, keen insight, and sound judgment. Wisdom is related to knowledge in that wisdom is the ability to use knowledge properly. It is appropriate that Paul would mention wisdom as the first gift, because the Holy Spirit is the Spirit of wisdom (Ephesians 1:17). In the Old Testament, the Spirit of wisdom guided the hands of the craftsmen who were in charge of building the tabernacle and making the garments of the high priest (Exodus 28:3). The Spirit of wisdom also filled Joshua and gave him abilities for leadership (Deuteronomy 34:9). Isaiah prophesied that the Messiah would possess the Spirit of wisdom (Isaiah 11:2), which would enable him to rule over his kingdom with justice. In the Church, wisdom is needed on a daily basis so that leaders and members can make good decisions, especially in the area of the goals and purposes of the Church.

2. The word of knowledge. Knowledge is the apprehension of the truth; therefore, a word of knowledge is a revelation of truth. It may be knowledge of the Scripture, or it may be knowledge about the secrets of a person's heart (Mark 2:8; Luke 5:22). It is any kind of supernaturally obtained knowledge that does not come through study.

3. Faith. Faith is essentially trust in the Word of God. The gift of faith does not refer to the faith that we exhibit when we are saved. It refers to faith that is given to us by the Holy Spirit on a particular occasion so that the Church may be encouraged or blessed. Without faith, we make void the Word of God (Hebrews 4:2); but if we have faith, anything is possible (Mark 9:23; 11:20-24).

4. Gifts of healings. Healing is the process of making someone well. Gifts of healings refer to divine healings. The Holy Spirit gives to someone the "prayer of faith" (James 5:15), so that the sick can receive their healing. The word "gifts" is in the plural because there are all kinds of sicknesses and diseases (Matthew 4:23). This gift also includes the healing of mental illness, and the healing of the "brokenhearted" (Luke 4:18).

5. Working of miracles. Miracles are manifestations of God's power outside of natural law. Among other things, miracles include casting out devils and raising the dead. Healings are also a type of miracle, a fact that demonstrates how the gifts of the Spirit are interrelated and overlapping. Jesus performed many miracles, such as turning water into wine (John 2:3-11), walking on water (Matthew 14:25), and multiplying the bread and fish (Mark 6:38-44). We read in the book of Acts that God worked "unusual miracles by the hands of Paul" (Acts 19:11).

6. Prophecy. Prophecy is any kind of message that is revealed to us supernaturally by God. It may include facts related to the past, the present, or the future. The prophetic message usually calls the Church to repentance or obedience. It may point the Church in new directions. Regarding the purpose of prophecy, Paul writes, "he who prophesies speaks edification and exhortation and comfort to men" (1 Corinthians 14:3).

7. Discerning of spirits. The word "discerning" means to judge the true nature of something. Therefore, discerning of spirits is the divinely given ability to judge the true nature of a "spirit." The presence of spiritual gifts in the Church requires also the ability to discern the genuineness of those gifts. John advises us, "Beloved, do not believe every spirit, but test the spirits, whether they are of

God; because many false prophets have gone out into the world"
(1 John 4:1).

8. Different kinds of tongues. The word "tongues" means "languages," and there are thousands of languages in the world. However, the Holy Spirit is able to communicate in all of those languages, and he can give to any believer the ability to speak in any of those languages. The gift of tongues does not refer to learning a language; it refers to a supernatural gift of language.

9. The interpretation of tongues. In order for the gift of tongues to benefit the whole church, the tongues must be interpreted. Therefore, when someone speaks in tongues, God gives the interpretation to one or more persons in the congregation. Sometimes, the person who speaks also receives the interpretation (1 Corinthians 14:13). If someone speaks in tongues, but no one is given the interpretation, the speaker should then be quiet and speak only to God so that the worship service is not interrupted (1 Corinthians 14:28). The private use of tongues should never be forbidden (1 Corinthians 14:39).

Each of these gifts is distributed in the Church as God wills. We are not allowed to choose which gifts we want. If we desire spiritual gifts, we must make ourselves available by prayer, fasting, obedience, and study of God's Word.

d. Every gift is important to the body
Just as our human body has many parts, so also the Body of Christ is made up of many different members. We should appreciate the diversity of the Body while working always for the unity of the Body.

> For as the body is one and has many members, but all the
> members of that one body, being many, are one body, so also
> is Christ" (1 Corinthians 12:12).

The Church is the Body of Christ, and the head of the body is Christ (Colossians 1:18). The Body of Christ has a unity of purpose, as directed by Christ the head (1 Corinthians 12:25). Every part of the body cares for every other part of the body. Every part of the Body of Christ is needed; and no part should exalt itself above another. Good leaders encourage unity in the body, respect for each member, and utilization of all the gifts. Members must be nurtured, trained, and released to minister.

e. We should seek for the spiritual gifts

The gifts of the Spirit enable the Church to worship God fully and effectively. Therefore, we should desire spiritual gifts and we should surrender our lives to the LORD so that he can use us. Paul writes:

> "But earnestly desire the best gifts. And yet I show you a more excellent way" (1 Corinthians 12:31). "Pursue love, and desire spiritual gifts, but especially that you may prophesy" (1 Corinthians 14:1).

f. Spiritual gifts are not proof of spiritual maturity

Paul states that the church at Corinth was blessed with many spiritual gifts. He says to them "you come short in no gift" (1 Corinthians 1:7). That is, there is no other church with more spiritual gifts. At the same time, however, the Corinthians had severe spiritual deficiencies, so much so that Paul refers to them as "carnal." He writes, "And I, brethren, could not speak to you as to spiritual people but as to carnal, as to babes in Christ" (1 Corinthians 3:1). Therefore, although spiritual gifts have an important role in the Church and in worship, they do not take the place of maturity, holiness, or the fruit of the Spirit.

D. Liberty in the Spirit

1. The Spirit gives freedom in worship

Worship in the Spirit allows for the freedom and the movement of the Holy Spirit. The apostle Paul states, "Now the LORD is the Spirit; and where the Spirit of the LORD is, there is liberty" (2 Corinthians 3:17). Worship in the Spirit is motivated and moved by the Holy Spirit, and it is empowered by the Holy Spirit. The liberty of worship in the Spirit means that the Church is not limited by formalism or ritualism. We allow the Holy Spirit to direct the worship and to change the order of service. Worship in the Spirit gives liberty in praise, liberty in prayer, and liberty to rejoice. In the Spirit, we have liberty to "shout for joy and be glad" (Psalm

35:27). We have liberty to "praise His name with the dance" (Psalm 149:3).

2. Liberty is not chaos

Worship in the Spirit produces liberty for every kind of spiritual manifestation. However, liberty always has a purpose and a goal. The Spirit gives liberty so that the Church may minister to one another and reach out to unbelievers. Therefore, the liberty of the Spirit has certain boundaries. Paul writes, "Let all things be done decently and in order" (1 Corinthians 14:40). Liberty must not be allowed to degenerate into chaos. The members of the body must submit to the Head, which is Christ; and Christ has put into place the pastors and leaders who oversee the worship. God has a plan and a purpose for every church and for every worship service. Ultimately, the Spirit works for unity in the Body of Christ so that believers will be in "one accord" (Acts 2:1).

Conclusion

The Pentecostal church has a long history of powerful worship in which the Holy Spirit is present and lives are changed. Unfortunately, many of our churches are now satisfied to continue week after week without the genuine moving of the Holy Spirit. When the Holy Spirit is no longer moving in our worship, we then attempt to create a spiritual atmosphere by mere human efforts. We create the smoke, but we have no fire. We settle for shallow worship where the emphasis is on entertainment. We have an outward display but no inward power. We become like the ancient Israelites who were rebuked by Jeremiah. He wrote, "you have forsaken the fountain of living water, and you have carved out for yourselves cisterns, broken cisterns that hold no water" (Jeremiah 2:13). The LORD himself was Israel's fountain of living water, but when they forsook the LORD, they had to create substitutes. Therefore, they carved out cisterns for holding water, but their manmade cisterns had cracks, and they would hold no water. Likewse, nothing that we do can replace the genuine presence of God. We become like those of whom Paul spoke, when he wrote, "having a form of godliness but denying the power thereof" (2 Timothy 3:5).

The days in which we live were predicted by the apostle Paul: "Now the Spirit speaketh expressly, that in the latter times some shall depart from the faith" (1 Timothy 4:1). It is time that we wake up from our sleep and return to the kind of worship that pleases God. The first step in that return is to repent (Isaiah 1:16-20). Like the Church at Ephesus, we must return to our first love. Jesus said,

> Nevertheless I have somewhat against thee, because thou hast left thy first love. Remember therefore from whence thou art fallen, and repent, and do the first works; or else I will come unto thee quickly, and will remove thy candlestick out of his place, except thou repent (Revelation 2:4-5).

There is no easy pathway to regain the ground that we have lost. We must humble ourselves before the LORD in fasting and prayer. We must wait upon the LORD until he comes and once again pours out his Spirit upon us.

Questions for Review and Application

1. Describe the Holy Spirit as "the fuel of worship".

2. Read the Gospel of John chapters 1-4 and list every reference to the Holy Spirit.

3. In John 4, what does Jesus say about the location of worship?

4. Explain how the Samaritan faith was incomplete and insufficient.

5. What has Jehovah done to deserve our worship?

6. Name the ways that our theology is involved in our worship.

7. Why is it necessary to worship God in spirit and truth?

8. How does the Holy Spirit help us to worship?

9. What can we do to welcome and encourage the Holy Spirit's presence in our worship?

10. Describe the relationship between the Holy Spirit and rejoicing.

11. What is "praying in the Spirit"?

12. Explain how Joel's prophecy (Joel 2:28-29) relates to worship "in the Spirit."

13. Define the term "spiritual gifts".

14. Peter makes four points regarding spiritual gifts. List them.

    (1)

    (2)

    (3)

    (4)

15. List the spiritual gifts that are found in Romans 12.

16. What is the purpose of the ministry gifts that are named in Ephesians 4:7-13?

17. What is Paul's main point in 1 Corinthians 12:1?

18. Describe the threefold working of the gifts.

19. List and define the nine spiritual gifts found in 1 Corinthians 12: 8-11:

    (1)

    (2)

    (3)

    (4)

    (5)

    (6)

    (7)

    (8)

    (9)

20. How do we balance liberty in the Spirit with the necessary order in worship?

CHAPTER 7

COMPONENTS OF A WORSHIP SERVICE (PART 1)

And let us consider one another in order to stir up love and good works, not forsaking the assembling of ourselves together, as is the manner of some, but exhorting one another, and so much the more as you see the Day approaching (Hebrews 10:24-25).

The threefold goal of worship is to honor God, strengthen the Church, and impact the world. If these three objectives are to be accomplished in our worship, then we must follow the biblical pattern for worship. In the next two chapters, we will discuss the seven essential components of an effective worship service: 1. Powerful prayer, 2. Meaningful music, 3. Passionate praise, 4. Tithing and giving, 5. Preaching the Word, 6. Teaching the Word, and 7. Personal testimonies. Each of these seven elements of worship contributes to the purposes and goals of worship.

A. Powerful prayer

1. The priority of prayer

a. Prayer was a priority in the Old Testament temple
Old Testament temple worship is often described in terms of rituals and sacrifices. However, prayer was also an important part of Old Testament worship. When King Solomon dedicated the new temple, the LORD responded by filling the house with his glory. Then the LORD spoke to Solomon and the people, saying,

Now My eyes will be open and My ears attentive to prayer made in this place. For now I have chosen and sanctified this house (2 Chronicles 7:15-16).

The LORD's promise demonstrates that he was not interested so much in the burnt offerings, sacrifices, and the rituals. Instead, the LORD spoke of his house as a "chosen and sanctified" place where prayers would be answered.

b. Jesus taught the priority of prayer

Jesus taught his disciples that prayer was a priority for the individual believer and for the Church. Jesus' emphasis on prayer caused him to utter a powerful remark concerning the purpose of the Church. Jesus said, "Is it not written, 'My house shall be called a house of prayer for all nations'?" (Mark 11:17). What comes to mind when we say the word "Church"? It is common today for the Church to be called a house of worship, a house of preaching, a house of fellowship, a house of service, or a house of music. However, Jesus insisted that the Church should be a "house of prayer for all nations." Without sincere prayer, worship is empty. Without prayer, the Church cannot fulfill its mission in the world.

c. Paul taught the priority of prayer

The apostle Paul affirms very strongly the priority of prayer in worship. Writing to Timothy, Paul gives instructions for the proper conduct of worship. Paul begins with this command:

Therefore I exhort first of all that supplications, prayers, intercessions, and giving of thanks be made for all men ... I desire therefore that the men pray everywhere, lifting up holy hands, without wrath and doubting (1 Timothy 2:1-8).

When describing the worship service, Paul emphasizes prayer "first of all." Along with the ministries of music and preaching, the ministry of prayer is a powerful aspect of the Church's influence in the world.

d. The early church practiced the priority of prayer

Prayer was a vital part of worship in the early church. Even before the Holy Spirit was poured out on the Day of Pentecost, the disciples gathered for worship, and they "all continued with one accord in **prayer** and supplication" (Acts 1:14). After Pentecost, the disciples, along with the 3,000 new converts, "continued steadfastly in the apostles' doctrine and fellowship, in the breaking of bread, and in **prayers**" (Acts 2:42). The apostles attended the prayer services in the temple daily (Acts 3:1; 6:4; 22:17), and the Church gathered for special times of prayer (Acts 4:31). On one occasion, they prayed for Peter's deliverance from prison (Acts 12:5, 12). They prayed and fasted for God's anointing upon missionaries and leaders (Acts 6:6; 13:3; 14:23). Prayer was an important element of every worship service (1 Corinthians 12:4, 5, 13), including prayer in tongues (1 Corinthians 14:13, 14, 15).

2. The kinds of prayer

In his instructions to Timothy, Paul mentions different kinds of prayer: "supplications, prayers, intercessions." Along with these three categories, the New Testament speaks of prayer in terms of asking, seeking, invocation, and petition. The most common Greek term that is translated as **prayer** is *proseuche*, which is used for all types of prayer. The variety of other New Testament terms suggests that the following types of prayer should be offered during worship services:

a. Invocation (Greek epiklesis)

An invocation is a prayer that calls upon the LORD to answer. Normally, we speak of invocation as the opening prayer that calls upon God to be present in the worship service and to bless the Church's time together (1 Peter 1:17; Acts 2:21).

b. Petition or request (Greek aitema)

A petition or request is prayer for a specific need. Every Church should post a list of needs that the members can use to guide their petitions. This would include prayer for the sick. Paul writes, "Be careful for nothing; but in every thing by prayer and supplication with thanksgiving let your **requests** be made known unto God" (Philippians 4:6).

c. Intercession (Greek enteuxis)

Intercession is a prayer that is offered on behalf of someone else. (1 Timothy 2:1; 4:5; Hebrews 7:25). The Church's intercession should include prayer for the lost because God "desires all men to be saved and to come to the knowledge of the truth" (1 Timothy 2:4).

d. Supplication (Greek deesis)

A supplication is a prayer that is offered with urgency and passion because of the great need. Paul advises us to be "praying always with all prayer and supplication in the Spirit, being watchful to this end with all perseverance and supplication for all the saints" (Ephesians 6:18).

3. The manner of prayer

Prayer may be offered up to God in a variety of ways. At certain points in the service, individuals may pray on behalf of the congregation or on behalf of special needs. However, prayer is a ministry of all the people; therefore, every believer should participate in prayer. The early church practiced what may be called "concert prayer," which means that everyone prays aloud together in unison. An example is found in Acts 4:24, which reads,

> So when they heard that, they raised their voice to God with one accord and said: "LORD, You are God, who made heaven and earth and the sea, and all that is in them ...".

God can hear and understand everyone's prayers at once, and the surrounding noise creates a "prayer closet," in which each person calls upon God according to their own needs and desires.

The worship service should also include times for people to "seek the LORD" (Hosea 10:12), "pour out" their souls to the LORD (1 Samuel 1:15), and "wait upon the LORD" (Isaiah 40:31). These more lengthy prayer times can come at the end of the service when people pray in the altar, or they can be part of special prayer services or take place in a designated prayer room in the church.

4. The necessity of prayer

In the past, Pentecostal churches would have worship services on Sunday morning, Sunday evening, and Wednesday evening. In addition to these regular services, they would often have weekly prayer services and regular revival meetings that might last a week or more. During many of these worship services, particularly on Sunday evenings and during revivals, prayer was one of the most important elements of the service. People would often gather for prayer before the services, and then they would spend extended times of prayer and waiting upon the LORD in the altar at the end of the services. There in the altar, people would pray one for another. Sinners and backsliders would receive Jesus as their Savior. People who were struggling with bondages and bad habits would receive Jesus as their sanctifier. Believers who were hungry for more of the power of God in their lives would the baptized in the Holy Spirit. The church would lay hands upon the sick and they would recover.

Today, however, many of our churches present very little opportunity for people to wait upon the LORD and seek his face. Some churches no longer have a Sunday evening service, and many no longer have revival meetings. Therefore, if Christians are to pray, they must do it alone and in their own homes. Although solitary prayer is important, there is no substitute for the added power that comes when God's people pray together and pray one for another. If the Pentecostal church is to have revival and is to impact modern society, then we must make time for prayer, for seeking the face of God, for intercession, and for waiting upon the LORD together, until God once again pours out his Spirit upon us.

B. Meaningful music

Biblical descriptions of worship consistently include music. By music, I mean singing and playing musical instruments. The first biblical reference to music is found in the book of Genesis. Jubal, one of the sons of Lamech, is said to be "the father of all those who play the harp and flute" (Genesis 4:21). In the final book of the Bible, we read about the people of God in heaven, "standing on the sea of glass, having harps of God. They sing the song of Moses, the servant of God, and the song of the Lamb" (Revelation 15:2-3). Between Genesis and Revelation, we find hundreds of examples of men, women, and children who worship God through one form of music or another.

1. The Holy Spirit and music

The apostle Paul makes a direct connection between being filled with the Spirit and worshiping God through music and singing. He writes,

> And do not be drunk with wine, in which is dissipation; but be filled with the Spirit, speaking to one another in psalms and hymns and spiritual songs, singing and making melody in your heart to the LORD, giving thanks always for all things to God the Father in the name of our LORD Jesus Christ (Ephesians 5:18-20).

The definitions of psalms, hymns, and spiritual songs are not entirely clear, but the three terms suggest that God is pleased with a variety of music. Paul is saying that there are different kinds of songs, and each type of song has its place in worship. So how do we decide what kind of music to sing and which songs to sing? First, our songs should reflect the biblical teachings about God and the spiritual life. Songs should be faithful to biblical teaching. Second, the music should glorify God. Third, the music should draw people into worship.

2. Commands to sing to the LORD

Music and singing are not optional. The LORD takes pleasure in our worship, and he instructs us to sing unto him. The following verses are only a small sample of the numerous biblical commands for us to sing unto the LORD:

> Sing to the LORD, all the earth; Proclaim the good news of His salvation from day to day (1 Chronicles 16:23).

> Sing praise to the LORD, You saints of His, And give thanks at the remembrance of His holy name (Psalm 30:4).

> Oh come, let us sing to the LORD! Let us shout joyfully to the Rock of our salvation (Psalm 95:1).

> Oh, sing to the LORD a new song! For He has done marvelous things; His right hand and His holy arm have gained Him the victory (Psalm 98:1).

Sing to the LORD, For He has done excellent things; This *is* known in all the earth (Isaiah 12:5).

Sing to the LORD! Praise the LORD! For He has delivered the life of the poor From the hand of evildoers (Jeremiah 20:13).

3. Music in heavenly worship

Singing was a prominent feature in John's vision of heavenly worship. The inhabitants of heaven sang in worship of the Lamb of God:

> And they sang a new song, saying:
>> You are worthy to take the scroll,
>>> And to open its seals;
>> For You were slain,
>>> And have redeemed us to God by Your blood
>> Out of every tribe and tongue and people and nation
>>> (Revelation 5:9).

John explains that only the redeemed are able to sing the new song:

> They sang as it were a new song before the throne, before the four living creatures, and the elders; and no one could learn that song except the hundred and forty-four thousand who were redeemed from the earth (Revelation 14:3).

4. The Psalms and music

The Psalms may be read, recited, or chanted, but they were originally meant to be sung, a fact that testifies to the value of music in worship. The Hebrew word *mizmor*, translated 'psalm', is 'a song sung to an instrumental accompaniment', and its root word, *zamar*, encompasses the broad idea of "making music." These terms are found 106 times in the Old Testament. The Old Testament, therefore, places heavy emphasis upon music as a part of worship. Old Testament scholar Sigmund Mowinckel observes that in all ancient worship, "song, music and dance play an important role."[21]

Some people believe that music is just a preliminary activity that leads to more important parts of the service, such as preaching

---

[21] Sigmund Mowinckel, *The Psalms in Israel's Worship* (2 vols.; New York: Abingdon Press, 1967), p. 8.

or the Eucharist. However, the Bible teaches that worship through song is an end in itself and that singing does not necessarily lead to another part of worship.

5. Pentecostal music

The significant role of music in the Pentecostal tradition can hardly be overstated. In their book on global Pentecostalism, Donald E. Miller and Tetsunao Yamamori offer the following insight: 'Whether in a storefront building with bare florescent tubes hanging from the ceiling or in a theater with a sophisticated sound system, the heart of Pentecostalism is the music'.[22] Harvey Cox, in his celebrated study of Pentecostalism, devotes an entire chapter to the importance of music; and regarding Pentecostalism's openness to a broad variety of musical styles, Cox observes,

> Most pentecostals gladly welcome any instrument you can blow, pluck, bow, bang, scrape, or rattle in the praise of God. I have seen photos of saxophones being played at pentecostal revivals as early as 1910 ... I have heard congregations sing to the beat of salsa, bossa nova, country western, and a dozen other tempos.[23]

The Pentecostal emphasis upon music is affirmed by the presence of the book of Psalms within the Bible – 150 songs (not to mention the other songs scattered throughout Scripture). In light of the Psalms, I would argue that songs can function as the Word of God just as surely as preaching can. God speaks to the Church through preaching, but God speaks through music also.

C. Passionate praise

1. Thanksgiving and praise

Worship is the expression of our love relationship and consecration to God. Although worship is a lifestyle, there are also special

---

[22] Miller and Yamamori, *Global Pentecostalism: The New Face of Christian Social Engagement* (Berkeley, CA: University of California Press, 2007), pp. 23-24.

[23] Harvey G. Cox, *Fire from Heaven: The Rise of Pentecostal Spirituality and the Reshaping of Religion in the 21st Century* (London: Cassell, 1996), pp. 142-43.

moments of worship when we direct our thoughts, our praises, and our thanksgiving to God. We come into God's presence with thanksgiving, singing his praises. In his presence, we worship him intimately with the highest of intentions, setting our mind on things above and not on earthly things.

Our expressions of thanksgiving, praise, and worship are the only things we can give to God that he did not create. The time in a worship service that is dedicated to offering thanksgiving, praise, and worship to God is very pleasing to him.

The Bible presents two primary categories or types of praise, expressed by two Hebrew terms, *hallal* and *yadah*. On the one hand, *yadah*, translated "give thanks," signifies praising God for what he has done. Thanksgiving is an expression of gratitude for God's mighty works. It is giving thanks to God for what he has done in our lives, and, more specifically, for answers to prayer. On the other hand, *hallal*, translated "praise," signifies praising God for his character and attributes. Praise, then, is a statement that acknowledges and celebrates God's character and attributes. We praise God for who he is (for example, Psalm 150)!

a. Thanksgiving

Thanksgiving is the expression of gratitude to God for all that he has done and for all he has promised in his Word. It is easy to complain; and if we make a habit of complaining, we will find it a very difficult habit to break. Every year, we celebrate holidays that reminds us to look on the bright side of things, to appreciate what God has done for us, and to draw close to our family and friends. However, the practice of giving thanks must not be confined to one or two days per year. We should express our gratitude to God continually. The apostle Paul tells us, "in everything give thanks; for this is the will of God in Christ Jesus for you (1 Thessalonians 5:18).

In the Old Testament, God blessed the Israelites with a land flowing with milk and honey. Just as God blessed Israel, he has blessed us. He has given us the promise of a heavenly city that we did not build, with an inheritance that we did not provide. We drink from the well of his Spirit, and we eat the fruit of his Word. By his grace he has saved us, healed us, kept us, provided for us, and he will continue to do so. God has blessed us with all spiritual blessings in the heavenly places. He has made us partakers of his glory. He has called us to be his beloved children. He has given us the joy that passes all understanding. He has not left us orphans, but he has given us a constant companion in the Holy Spirit. For all of these things, we give thanks.

b. Praise

Praise is acknowledging and celebrating the person of God. We praise him for who he is. Praise is not based on our feelings or our moods. We do not praise God only when we feel like it. Praise is a choice of our will. We must choose to praise the LORD, and we must be determined to praise the LORD. Our praise is offered because of God's greatness, and God's greatness never changes. Praise comes to us easily whenever we think about the greatness of God, his character, and his actions. Praise creates an atmosphere that is welcoming to the presence of God. The psalmist wrote that God is "enthroned on the praises of Israel" (Psalm 22:3).

God is majestic and exalted, the King of kings, the LORD of lords, and the God of gods; therefore, he is worthy of praise. God created the heaven, the earth, the angels, and all of humanity; therefore, he is worthy of praise. Not only is God majestic in holiness, but God is also loving, kind, and compassionate. The goal of worship is praise; therefore, the Psalter concludes with a hymn of praise that declares "Let everything that has breath praise the LORD" (Psalm 150:6).

Praise is a natural part of human life. When we listen to a beautiful song that is sung by a talented vocalist and accompanied by accomplished musicians, we stand in awe, and we offer our applause. We praise the singer, the songwriter, and the musicians. When we view a magnificent work of art, we offer praise to the artist. When we feast upon a well-cooked meal, we praise the cook. Praise is natural. When we think upon the nature of God and his incomparable attributes, we should praise him. When we remember his acts of kindness and his gracious forgiveness, we should praise him.

When we praise God, we are focusing our energy toward God and his goodness rather than toward ourselves and our problems. When we praise God, we are acknowledging that God is our source of life, our source of joy, and our source of peace. When we praise God, we are declaring that God is our savior, redeemer, and intercessor, who is able to keep us from falling.

2. Exuberant praise

When I first came into Pentecostalism, I observed the general loudness, exuberance, and physical involvement in Pentecostal worship, as well as more specific Pentecostal practices like shouting, leaping, dancing, clapping, lifting the hands, and the use of musical instruments like the tambourine (see Psalms 81:3; 149.3; 150.4).

Even if it is not a part of our normal personality to be exuberant, we must try to be exuberant in our praise. Some of us are quiet by nature, but even quiet people, on occasion, should express their praises to God with a loud voice. We are told to "Shout to God with the voice of triumph" (Psalm 47;1) and to "make a joyful noise unto the LORD" (Psalm 100:1). When the church is worshiping together, it is appropriate for us to praise God with a loud voice. Whether we feel like it or whether we do not feel like it, we must make a sacrifice of praise. If we do not praise him, "the rocks will cry out." We must open our mouths and tell God that we love him. Worship is an expression of our love for God. If we are unable to express our affection for God, then we are missing out on a great blessing. At times, even an introverted person needs to be expressive, and the extroverted person needs to be quiet.

3. Expressions of praise

In addition to the expression of praise through music and singing, there are many other biblical ways to give praise to God.

a. Lifting our hands

Lifting the hands is a sign of submission, of yearning, of longing, and of affection. Lifting the hands is also a sign of receiving from God. The Old Testament believers lifted their hands in praise to God: "And Ezra blessed the LORD, the great God. Then all the people answered, 'Amen, Amen!' while lifting up their hands" (Nehemiah 8:6). We are commanded in the Psalms, "Lift up your hands in the sanctuary" (Psalm 134:2; also 28.2; 63.5). In the New Testament, the apostle Paul advises us to lift our hands in worship: "I desire therefore that the men pray everywhere, lifting up holy hands, without wrath and doubting" (1 Timothy 2:8).

b. Clapping our hands

While lifting our hands is a sign of surrender and longing, we are also told to clap our hands as a sign of praise and acclamation. "Clap your hands all you peoples; shout unto God with the voice of triumph" (Psalm 47:1). Clapping the hands is a part of celebrating the works of God.

c. Shouting

Shouting has been a particularly common expression of worship in Pentecostal services. It is a thoroughly biblical practice that is mentioned many times in Scripture. David said, "Shout for joy, all you upright in heart!" (Psalm 32:11).[24] Shouting symbolizes victory, as we can see in the story of Israel's defeat of Jericho. When the people shouted unto God, the walls of Jericho fell down (Joshua 6).

d. Dancing

Not only can praise be expressed vocally, it can also be expressed bodily. Dancing is a biblical method of praise. After they were delivered from Egyptian bondage, the Israelites praised God in music and song. Also, "Miriam the prophetess, the sister of Aaron, took the timbrel in her hand; and all the women went out after her with timbrels and with dances" (Exodus 15:20). When King David brought the Ark of the Covenant into Jerusalem, he celebrated with dancing. We read, "Then David danced before the LORD with all his might" (2 Samuel 6:14). In Psalm 150, David commands us, saying, "Praise Him with the ... dance" (150:4; also 30.11; 149.3). The biblical examples show that dancing can be spontaneous, or it

---

[24] In regard to shouting, see also Pss. 47:2; 65:14; 66:1; 81:1; 95:1, 2; 98:4, 6; 100:1 (Hebrew *rua*); 5:11; 20:6; 32:11; 17:1; 30:6; 33:1; 35:27; 42:5; 47:2; 51:16; 59:17; 61:2; 63:8; 65:9; 67:5; 71:23; 81:1; 84:3; 88:3; 89:13; 90:14; 92:5; 95:1; 96:12; 98:4; 98:8; 105:43; 106:44; 107:22; 118:15; 119:169; 126:2, 5; 132:9; 132:16; 142:7; 145:7; 149:5 (Hebrew *ranan*). Verse numbering follows the Hebrew text.

can be a planned event that utilizes trained dancers whose ministry inspires others to worship.

e. Standing

In the Old Testament Temple, there were no chairs and no pews. The priests stood continually before the LORD as they ministered to God (See 2 Chronicles 5:12; 7:6; 29:26; Psalm 135:2; Revelation 4:9-11). The posture of standing signifies two things. First, standing signifies respect. We stand to our feet when an important person enters the room. We stand on our feet as we sing the national anthem. We stand to our feet when the judge enters the courtroom. Second, standing signifies alertness. Standing and praising go together, because when we are standing, we are more inclined to participate in the worship.

f. Kneeling, bowing

In the Old Testament, the psalmist invites us: "Come, let us bow down and worship, let us kneel before the LORD our maker" (Psalm 95:6). In the New Testament, we read that "The twenty-four elders and the four living creatures fell down and worshiped God, who was seated upon the throne" (Revelation 19:4). Falling down in prostration is the most common form of worship that is found in the book of Revelation. We often sing about bowing before the LORD, but we rarely actually do it. Bowing signifies humility and submission. Kneeling and bowing also signify respect, which in the Bible is called the fear of the LORD.

g. Speaking in tongues

Jesus explained to the Samaritan woman that true worshipers must worship the Father "in Spirit and in Truth." As we worship in the Spirit, we will often praise God in unknown tongues, just as the disciples did on the Day of Pentecost. After the Holy Spirit fell upon them and they were "filled with the Holy Spirit," they went out into the streets of Jerusalem. People from every nation were there celebrating the annual feast. These foreigners said, "we hear them speaking in our own tongues the wonderful works of God" (Acts 2:11). The disciples were praising God in other tongues. This is what Paul means when he writes, "For he who speaks in a tongue does not speak to men but to God" (1 Corinthians 14:2).

Conclusion

In this chapter, we have talked about prayer, music, and praise as essential components of an effective worship service. In the next chapter, we will examine tithing and giving, preaching the Word, teaching the Word, and Personal testimonies.

Questions for Review and Application

1. List the seven components of an effective worship service.

2. Read 2 Chronicles 7:1-5 and summarize its emphasis on the subject of prayer.

3. If God's house is a house of prayer, what can we do to make prayer more meaningful?

4. Read 1 Timothy 2:1-8 and comment on the importance of prayer.

5. Write out the following Bible verses:

   Acts 3:1

   Acts 12:5

   Acts 14:23

   1 Corinthians 14:13

6. List and define four kinds of prayer.

   (1)

   (2)

   (3)

   (4)

7. What factors have contributed to the decline in prayer as a part of worship services?

8. Write out Revelation 15:2-3.

9. Explain the connection between the Holy Spirit and music as found in Ephesians 5:18-20.

10. Search your Bible for two Scriptures that command us to sing. Write them out.

11. Does music always serve as a prelude to other parts of worship, or is itself music valuable?

12. The book of Psalms consists of 150 songs. What does this fact say to us about the value of music?

13. What is the only thing that we can give to God that he did not make?

14. Describe the two primary categories of praise.

15. Explain why quiet people need to express their praises to God aloud.

16. List and explain seven ways that we express praise to God.

(1)

(2)

(3)

(4)

(5)

(6)

(7)

CHAPTER 8

COMPONENTS OF A WORSHIP SERVICE (PART 2)

And I, brethren, when I came to you, did not come with excellence of speech or of wisdom declaring to you the testimony of God. For I determined not to know anything among you except Jesus Christ and Him crucified ... And my speech and my preaching were not with persuasive words of human wisdom, but in demonstration of the Spirit and of power, that your faith should not be in the wisdom of men but in the power of God (1 Corinthians 2:1-5).

In the previous chapter, we identified the following seven components as essential parts of an effective worship service: 1. Powerful prayer, 2. Meaningful music, 3. Passionate praise, 4. Tithing and giving, 5. Preaching the Word, 6. Teaching the Word, and 7. Personal testimonies. Each of these seven elements of worship contributes to the goal of worship, which is to honor God, strengthen the Church, and impact the world. Having already discussed the first three items, we will begin this chapter with the fourth item – Tithing and Giving.

A. Tithing and giving

1. Worship is our gift to God

Worship is a gift – it is our gift to God – a gift of love, gratitude, commitment, and trust. One element of worship involves our giving back to God a portion of the material goods that he has placed in our hands. In the Old Testament, the Israelites were told always to bring their tithes and offerings to the house of God. If they were very poor, they were required to bring only a small gift; but if they were wealthy, they had to bring a larger gift. Be it large or small, they were always to bring a gift in their hands.

2. All things belong to God

Underlying the practice of tithing and giving is the truth that all things belong to God. The LORD said to Israel, "… all the earth is Mine" (Exodus 19:5); and again he said, "the land is Mine; for you are strangers and sojourners with Me" (Leviticus 25:23). The earth is the LORD's, and we are his stewards. He has given us all material goods so that we might use them for his glory. When we give to God, we are confessing that everything belongs to God. The LORD spoke to Job saying, "Everything under heaven is Mine" (Job 41:11); and in the Psalms we read,

> For every beast of the forest is Mine,
>   And the cattle on a thousand hills.
> I know all the birds of the mountains,
>   And the wild beasts of the field are Mine.
> If I were hungry, I would not tell you;
>   For the world is Mine, and all its fullness (Psalm 50:10-12).

Because everything belongs to the LORD, he asks that we give to him the tithe. He said, "And all the tithe of the land, whether of the seed of the land or of the fruit of the tree, is the LORD's. It is holy to the LORD" (Leviticus 27:30). The word "tithe" means "tenth;" therefore, the tithe is ten percent of a person's income.

3. Tithing results in God's blessing

When we tithe, we give ten percent of our possessions back to God as a witness that he also owns the other ninety percent. In the book of Malachi, the LORD explains what happens when we tithe and what happens when we do not tithe. The LORD says,

> Will a man rob God? Yet you have robbed Me! But you say, In what way have we robbed You? In tithes and offerings. You are cursed with a curse, For you have robbed Me, Even this whole nation. Bring all the tithes into the storehouse, That there may be food in My house, And try Me now in this, Says the LORD of hosts, If I will not open for you the windows of heaven And pour out for you such blessing That there will not be room enough to receive it. And I will rebuke the devourer for your

sakes, So that he will not destroy the fruit of your ground, Nor shall the vine fail to bear fruit for you in the field, Says the LORD of hosts (Malachi 3:8-11).

The LORD explains that Israel has "robbed" God by not paying their tithes and by not giving proper offerings. The Hebrew word "to rob" means "to steal," "to cheat," or "to defraud;" and it is the same word that forms the root of the name "Jacob." Like Jacob stole his brother's blessing, these children of Jacob were stealing what belongs to the LORD.

Because of their greed and theft, they were "cursed" by God. In Hebrew, the repetition "cursed with a curse" is emphatic, and it means "you are indeed cursed" or "you are surely cursed." The effect of the curse is not stated, but the people would have been aware of the curses listed in Deuteronomy 28:15-24. Furthermore, it was not just a few of them who are guilty – it was the whole nation. Apparently, the withholding of the tithe was commonplace among the people in Malachi's day.

The LORD instructs the people to bring "all the tithes into the storehouse," that is, into the temple, so that the priests and Levites would have food to eat. Some of them may have been paying a part of the tithe and others may have been paying nothing at all, but the LORD asked for "all the tithes."

The LORD sets forth his command in the form of a promise. He tells the people to bring in the whole tithe and put the LORD to the test. He says, "Prove me now." To "prove" is to "test," so the LORD is saying that if the people will be obedient, he will "open the windows of heaven, and pour" out a blessing upon them. The blessing will be so great that they will not have room enough to receive it all. As part of the blessing, the LORD will protect their crops so that "the devourer" cannot destroy their produce and the grapes will not fall prematurely from the vines (3:11). The "devourer" probably refers to locusts. With God's blessing, their land will bring forth in abundance and their grape vines will produce record crops. The LORD wants us to know that tithing will result in the blessings of God.

4. Jesus encouraged tithing

The practice of tithing is encouraged by Jesus, who spoke to the Pharisees about their priorities. Jesus says, "But woe to you Pharisees! For you tithe mint and rue and all manner of herbs, and pass by justice and the love of God. These you ought to have done, without leaving the others undone" (Luke 11:42). The Pharisees "ought to" have given attention to justice and love. But, still, tithing is something they should not leave "undone."

5. Giving to God is a privilege

The apostle Paul, discussing the topic of giving in 2 Corinthians chapter 9, writes:

> He who sows sparingly will also reap sparingly, and he who sows bountifully will also reap bountifully. So let each one give as he purposes in his heart, not grudgingly or of necessity; for God loves a cheerful giver. And God is able to make all grace abound toward you, that you, always having all sufficiency in all things, may have an abundance for every good work (2 Corinthians 9:6-8).

Paul's word to the church at Corinth teaches us at least three important lessons. First, we are blessed in proportion to how much we give. Second, we should give freely and not because we feel forced to give. Third, God is able to supply all of our needs abundantly.

Giving has always been a part of worship. God expects us to give in proportion to our blessings. If all we have is one penny, then we should bring it and give it to God. God will bless us if we give it from the heart (see Luke 21:1-4). I have attended churches recently where they did not receive any offerings; but instead, they had a box beside the door, and the pastor said, "At the end of the service as you leave put your tithes and offerings in the box." But the giving had no place within the worship service itself. I believe such as practice is unbiblical, because our giving is not a matter of paying the bills. Giving is an act of worship; and as an act of worship, the tithing and giving should be included within the order of service whenever we worship.

B. Preaching the Word

1. Worship should include hearing God's Word

Worship is the central theme of the book of Psalms, and yet the first Psalm focuses on the Word of God. It states that for the righteous person, "his delight is in the law of the LORD, And in His law he meditates day and night" (Psalm 1:2). As the introduction to the Psalms, Psalm 1 suggests that right worship begins with a love for God's Word.

This affection for the Word of God is a key to worship. The writer of Psalm 119 declares, "Oh, how I love your law! It is my meditation all the day" (v. 97, cf. vv. 113, 127, 140, 163, and 165). Psalm 19 praises God's "law", "testimony", "precepts", "commandments", and "judgments", saying, "More desired are they than gold, yea, than much fine gold: sweeter also than honey and the honeycomb" (v. 10, cf. Psalm 119:72, 103). Through the use of other emotional terms, the hearer of the Psalms is encouraged to put the law "in his heart" (37:31; 40:8), to "rejoice" in the law (119:14, 111, 162), to "long for" God's precepts (119:40), to "rejoice" in his statutes (19:8), to "desire" his commandments (119:131), to "run" toward them (119:32), and to make them his "songs" (119:54). The hearer is told to "rejoice" and "be glad" because of God's judgments (Psalm 48:11; 97:8). The psalmist pleads longingly, "Open my eyes, that I may see wondrous things out of your law" (119:18, cf. v. 129). The feelings of the psalmist are similar to those of Jeremiah, who exclaims, "Your word was for me the joy and rejoicing of my heart" (Jeremiah 15:16).

2. Old Testament worship involved Scripture

The reading of Scripture, the preaching of Scripture, and the teaching of Scripture were important elements in the worship of Israel. Their love for the Word of God is evident throughout the Old Testament. For example, when the people returned from the Babylonian captivity, Ezra the scribe read the Scriptures in front of all the people. He recounts the following response of the people:

> And Ezra opened the book in the sight of all the people, for he was standing above all the people; and when he opened it, all the people stood up. And Ezra blessed the LORD, the great

God. Then all the people answered, "Amen, Amen!" while lifting up their hands. And they bowed their heads and worshiped the LORD with their faces to the ground (Nehemiah 8:5-6).

3. Preaching is important to New Testament worship

The preaching and teaching of Scripture is central to New Testament worship as well. The apostle Paul commands Timothy, a young pastor: "Preach the word! Be ready in season and out of season. Convince, rebuke, exhort, with all longsuffering and teaching. For the time will come when they will not endure sound doctrine" (2 Timothy 4:2-3).

4. Preaching is important to Pentecostal worship

Preaching has played a crucial role in the Pentecostal movement and continues to be a vital component of the Pentecostal experience. As an act of worship, Pentecostal preaching is more than the dissemination of information. Both the preacher and the congregation worship God during the act of preaching. Both the delivery and the reception of the Word of God generate worship. The joy and wonder of preaching emerge from the realization that the Word of God is being proclaimed! The apostle Paul writes, "…when you received the word of God which you heard from us, you welcomed it not as the word of men, but as it is in truth, the word of God" (1 Thessalonians 2:13).

Pentecostal preaching is not a one-dimensional act of communication in which the preacher is speaking only to the listeners and the listeners are hearing only the speaker. In Pentecostal worship, the preacher exercises a priestly function, standing between God and congregation. The preacher speaks for God; but, at the same time, the preacher is one of the worshipers, offering up a "sacrifice of praise" (Hebrews 13:15). Therefore, the act of preaching is an act of worship, in which the preacher stands in God's holy presence, with one eye on God and the other eye on the congregation, with one foot on earth and the other foot in heaven, with one hand reaching up to God and the other hand stretched out to the people. The people also worship – they look both to the preacher and to God as they yield to the Holy Spirit.

5. Preaching should be a work of the Spirit

When I think about the role of the Holy Spirit in preaching, the following activities come to mind immediately:

a. The Holy Spirit empowers

It was only after Jesus had been empowered by the Holy Spirit that he began his public ministry of preaching, teaching, and healing. He went down to the Jordan and was baptized by John, and when he came up out of the water, the Holy Spirit descended upon him in the form of a dove. Afterwards, he fasted for forty days and nights in the wilderness, while being tempted by the devil. At the end of the forty days, "Jesus returned in the power of the Spirit into Galilee ..." (Luke 4:14). The Spirit endowed Jesus with power (Greek *dunamis*) for ministry.

Similarly, after the resurrection of Jesus, his disciples did not preach until the Holy Spirit empowered them. Jesus commanded them to remain in the city, until they were clothed "with power from on high" (Luke 24:49). The promise was fulfilled on the day of Pentecost, when the disciples were baptized in the Holy Spirit. As soon as they emerged from the upper room, Peter preached fearlessly to the multitude. While natural human abilities are an advantage to the preacher, genuine spiritual effectiveness cannot be obtained without the power of the Holy Spirit.

b. The Holy Spirit authorizes

When Jesus returned from his forty days of fasting in the wilderness, he entered into the synagogue, and at the designated point of the service he read from the book of Isaiah: "The Spirit of the LORD is upon Me, because He has anointed Me to preach ..." (Luke 4:18). After reading his text, Jesus announced that it was fulfilled in his own ministry. Because Jesus is anointed by the Holy Spirit, his actions of announcing, preaching, and setting free are not mere symbols or empty proclamations – his preaching results in genuine forgiveness, healing, and liberty for those who receive his message.

The Pentecostal movement has traditionally placed a high value upon the spiritual authority that comes from the Spirit's anointing, and rightly so. The words of Spirit-authorized preachers carry with them the power of salvation, deliverance, and hope for people who are lost, bound, and confused.

c. The Holy Spirit teaches

The Spirit's teaching ministry extends to all believers, including preachers. Therefore, the Holy Spirit empowers, authorizes, and teaches the preacher. The teaching ministry of the Spirit is especially valuable to the preacher during the process of study and sermon preparation. The Holy Spirit will not lead into error. Our view of preaching, therefore, should acknowledge the Spirit's work in teaching and guiding both preacher and Church into the truth.

d. The Holy Spirit produces signs and wonders

The apostle Paul serves as a helpful model as we construct a Pentecostal theology of preaching. Although Paul was apparently a gifted and trained orator, he chose not to focus his efforts on human modes of argument and reasoning. He preferred to preach the gospel plainly and to allow the Holy Spirit to demonstrate the power of the gospel through signs and wonders. Paul writes to the Corinthian church:

> And I, brethren, when I came to you, did not come with excellence of speech or of wisdom declaring to you the testimony of God. For I determined not to know anything among you except Jesus Christ and Him crucified ... And my speech and my preaching were not with persuasive words of human wisdom, but in demonstration of the Spirit and of power, that your faith should not be in the wisdom of men but in the power of God (1 Corinthians 2:1-5).

Paul's preaching did not rely upon human wisdom but on demonstration of the Spirit and power. Paul uses similar words in writing to the Thessalonians: "For our gospel did not come to you in word only, but also in power, and in the Holy Spirit" (1 Thessalonians 1:5). Furthermore, he writes to the Romans: "in mighty signs and wonders, by the power of the Spirit of God ... I have fully preached the gospel of Christ" (Romans 15:19). Although Paul does not state the exact nature of the Spirit's demonstrations, they were apparently very powerful and convincing signs.

e. The Holy Spirit makes preaching effective

Paul's rejection of human models of persuasion suggests that we should grant priority to the Holy Spirit as the one who convinces the hearers of the truth of the gospel. It must be remembered, however, that the Spirit's work of convincing the world is accomplished through the human agency of preaching. Paul acknowledges that "the preaching of the cross … is the power of God" (1 Cor. 1.18). However, the effectiveness of the sermon cannot be judged by immediate responses; because the Holy Spirit is at work not only in the present but also in the future.

C. Teaching the Word

1. Worship should include teaching of Scripture

The house of God is a place for teaching (Acts 2:42). The prophet Isaiah indicated a clear connection between teaching and worship. He declared the following:

> Many people shall come and say, "Come, and let us go up to the mountain of the LORD, To the house of the God of Jacob; He will teach us His ways, And we shall walk in His paths." For out of Zion shall go forth the law, And the word of the LORD from Jerusalem (Isaiah 2:3).

2. We face a crisis in discipleship

The Church today is faced with a serious challenge in regard to discipleship. Our schedule of worship and other activities does not give enough time for teaching the Word of God effectively. This issue must be addressed if the Pentecostal church is to continue being Pentecostal.

The lack of time for biblical teaching is one of the negative effect of our condensed schedules of worship. If we are to worship the LORD in Spirit and in truth, then our worship must be based upon the Word of God. If people are to grow in the faith, then they must be taught the Word of God. Our sermons must be filled with the Word of God. Also, we must provide opportunities such as classes in which people can learn the Holy Scriptures.

3. The value of Sunday School

Over the last 100 years, the most reliable method for learning the Bible has been the Sunday school. However, many churches have abandoned the Sunday school. I readily admit that the Sunday school is not a divine institution, but if we eliminate the Sunday school, we must replace it with another teaching ministry.

There is no substitute for the systematic study of the Bible. The prophet Amos warned of a day when there would come a great famine, "not a famine of bread, nor a thirst for water, but of hearing the words of the LORD" (Amos 8:11). Without some plan for biblical instruction, our churches will grow anemic and people will have no faith, because "faith comes by hearing and hearing by the word of God" (Romans 10:17).

D. Personal testimonies

1. Testimony is one aspect of congregational involvement

The New Testament presents a model of worship that includes participation by the congregation. Paul writes, "Whenever you come together, each of you has a psalm, has a teaching, has a tongue, has a revelation, has an interpretation. Let all things be done for edification" (1 Corinthians 14:26).

2. Testimony was common in the Old Testament

Testimonies were common in the Old Testament. Whenever God answered prayer, a person would come with his or her family and friends to the temple. At the temple, an offering or sacrifice would be made in thanks to God, and a testimony would be given to commemorate the occasion in praise to God. People would share with all who were present that God had intervened in the life of the worshiper.

3. Testimonies should not be perfunctory

Personal testimonies can include stories of salvation, healing, deliverance, Spirit baptism, and answers to prayer. Testimonies should be timely and inspiring. They should be presented clearly and briefly. Depending upon the size of the church, testimonies can be utilized in a variety of ways. Small groups are an excellent setting for sharing personal testimonies. In a large worship service, the people who will testify are often chosen beforehand by the church leaders.

4. Testimonies are a valuable part of worship

The purpose of testimony is to glorify God and to encourage the congregation. God's purposes in bringing deliverance are incomplete without our testimony. Our children need to hear that God has answered our prayers. Our friends and family need to hear what God has done in our lives. Some churches have become very impersonal, and the members of the congregation no longer share their lives with each other. There is great value in sharing our testimonies with one another in the context of worship.

Questions for Review and Application

1. List the seven components of an effective worship service.

2. Describe how worship is our gift to God.

3. Explain Leviticus 25:23 in relation to who owns property.

4. According to Malachi 3:8-11, what is the penalty for failing to pay our tithes?

5. According to Malachi 3:8-11, what is the blessing for paying our tithes?

6. What did Jesus teach regarding tithing?

7. List the teachings of Paul in 2 Corinthians 9:6-8 regarding giving.

8. Explain the priority of God's Word in relation to Psalm 1.

9. List four Scriptures that illustrate the believer's love for the Word of God.

10. How does Nehemiah 8:5-6 demonstrate Israel's love and respect for the Word of God?

11. According to 2 Timothy 4:1-3, why is preaching important?

12. Explain how Pentecostal preaching is an act of worship.

13. List and describe the five ways that the Holy Spirit influences preaching.

(1)

(2)

(3)

(4)

(5)

14. Write out Acts 2:42.

15. Why do we have a crisis in discipleship?

16. How is Sunday School valuable?

17. Why are testimonies important as a part of worship?

18. How would you suggest that churches include testimonies in their worship services?

CHAPTER 9

SACRAMENTS AND CEREMONIES (PART 1)

Then Peter said to them, "Repent, and let every one of you be baptized in the name of Jesus Christ for the remission of sins; and you shall receive the gift of the Holy Spirit" (Acts 2:38).

A. Sacramental worship

1. Definition of 'Sacrament'

A sacrament is a ceremony or action that serves as an outward visible sign of an inward spiritual work. The sacraments are visible expressions of what the New Testament calls the "mystery" of the Kingdom of God. Jesus said to his disciples, "To you it has been given to know the **mystery** of the kingdom of God" (Mark 4:11). The apostle Paul speaks about the "mystery of Christ" (Colossians 4:3), the "mystery of the gospel" (Ephesians 6:19), and the "mystery of the faith" (1 Timothy 3:9). He writes further, "God willed to make known what are the riches of the glory of this **mystery** among the Gentiles: which is Christ in you, the hope of glory" (Colossians 1:27). The work of the Holy Spirit in the human heart is a mystery that can be experienced but never fully understood or explained. The sacraments provide a visible representation of the Spirit's mysterious work of grace. Therefore, sacraments are object lessons regarding the Christian faith. However, they go beyond object lessons, because the act of participation in the sacrament, when combined with faith, actually imparts grace to the participant. For this reason, John Wesley used the term "means of grace."

2. What are the sacraments

Most Protestant denominations agree that water baptism and the LORD's Supper are sacraments. Recent Pentecostal theologians have proposed five sacraments to correspond with the Fivefold Gospel:[1] 1. Water baptism is an outward sign of the Spirit's inward work of salvation (regeneration). 2. Footwashing is the outward sign of the Spirit's inward work of sanctification. 3. Speaking in tongues is the outward sign of the Spirit's inward work of Spirit baptism. 4. Anointing with oil is the outward sign of the Spirit's inward work of divine healing. 5. The LORD's Supper is the outward sign of the Spirit's inward work of hope and patience as we anticipate the return of our soon-coming King. Many Pentecostal churches name only water baptism and the LORD's Supper as sacraments. Some denominations also include footwashing as a sacrament. Still other denominations refer to these rituals only as **ordinances**, not sacraments.

We will be addressing the four rituals that can and should be placed on the church's calendar on a regular basis. The initial gift of speaking in tongues, however, cannot be planned according to human will; because we speak only as the Spirit gives the utterance (Acts 2:4). Nevertheless, we should allow the freedom in our worship services for those who have already been baptized in the Holy Spirit to operate in the gift of speaking in tongues. Thus, the sign of tongues should be encouraged in every worship service.

In addition to the practices of water baptism, footwashing, anointing with oil, and the LORD's Supper, we will also offer instruction regarding the dedication of children. Although child dedication is not a sacrament, it is an important ceremony in the lives of church families.

---

[1] See, for example, John Christopher Thomas, "Toward a Pentecostal Theology of Anointed Cloths," in Lee Roy Martin (ed.), *Toward a Pentecostal Theology of Worship* (Cleveland, TN: CPT Press, 2016), pp. 91-113.

B. Water baptism

1. The meaning of water baptism

Water baptism is the outward sacramental sign of the inward work of our salvation. This baptism represents our cleansing unto God. Baptism signifies that we have begun a new life. The apostle Paul states that we are "buried with Him through baptism into death, that just as Christ was raised from the dead by the glory of the Father, even so we also should walk in newness of life" (Romans 6:4). We have been buried with Christ and raised with him. Even Jesus recognized the need to be baptized in order to identify himself with the people of God (Matthew 3:13-17).

In the Scripture passage that we call The Great Commission, Jesus instructed us to baptize everyone who receives Christ as their savior. Jesus said, "Go therefore and make disciples of all the nations, baptizing them in the name of the Father and of the Son and of the Holy Spirit, teaching them to observe all things that I have commanded you" (Matthew 28:19-20).

The apostles were faithful to do as the LORD commanded them. We read in the book of Acts that Peter practiced water baptism. At the end of his sermon on the day of Pentecost, Peter gave his listeners the following clear directive:

Repent, and let every one of you be baptized in the name of Jesus Christ for the remission of sins; and you shall receive the gift of the Holy Spirit … Then those who gladly received his word were baptized; and that day about three thousand souls were added to them (Acts 2:38-41; see also Acts 8:12-13, 38; 9:18; 10:48; 16:15, 33; 18:8; 19:5).

We should encourage baptism as an act of obedience and as a celebration of the believer's new life. It is also a public testimony that we have been renewed. Water baptism, then, reminds us of the public and communal nature of the Christian life. New believers should be baptized soon after their conversion. However, it may be advisable for them first to complete a discipleship program to ensure that their conversion is genuine.

2. A water baptism service

The following service may be used, or it may be adapted to the needs and preferences of your congregation.

a. The Minister enters the water

The minister shall enter the water and the candidates for water baptism shall stand nearby, prepared to enter the water when called upon to do so.

b. Scripture reading

The minister addresses the congregation, reading one or more of the following Scriptures:

Hear the words of our LORD Jesus Christ:

> All authority has been given to Me in heaven and on earth. Go therefore and make disciples of all the nations, baptizing them in the name of the Father and of the Son and of the Holy Spirit, teaching them to observe all things that I have commanded you; and lo, I am with you always, even to the end of the age (Matthew 28:18-20).

> He who believes and is baptized will be saved; but he who does not believe will be condemned (Mark 16:16).

On the Day of Pentecost, Peter preached to the multitude, and when they asked what they must do in response to his sermon, he replied:

> Repent, and let every one of you be baptized in the name of Jesus Christ for the remission of sins; and you shall receive the gift of the Holy Spirit. For the promise is to you and to your children, and to all who are afar off, as many as the LORD our God will call (Acts 2:38-39).

The minister may also read one or more of the following: Ephesians 4:4-6; Galatians 3:27-28; Romans 6:3-4; John 1:12-13; Genesis 17:7; Galatians 3:29; Colossians 2:12; 1 Peter 3:20-21.

c. Teaching on the meaning of water baptism

The minister continues:

> Baptism is the sign and seal of God's promises to this covenant people.

In baptism God promises by grace alone:
to forgive our sins;
to adopt us into the Body of Christ, the Church;
to send the Holy Spirit daily to renew and cleanse us;
and to resurrect us to eternal life.

This promise is made visible in the water of baptism.

Water cleanses;
purifies;
refreshes;
sustains:
Jesus Christ is living water.

Through baptism Christ calls us to new obedience:
to love and trust God completely;
to forsake the evil of the world; and
to live a new and holy life.

d. Presentation of the Candidate

The minister shall invite each candidate to enter the water, and
say the following:

I present (*Name of Candidate*) to follow Christ in water baptism.

e. Profession of faith in Jesus Christ

The minister addresses the candidate:

Beloved of God,
you stand before us to follow Christ in water baptism.
I ask you, therefore, before God and Christ's church
to profess your faith in Christ Jesus.

Do you believe that Christ died for our sins?
That he was buried, and that he rose again on the third day?
Do you confess that you believe in Jesus Christ as your only
LORD and Savior?

(Candidate answers: I DO)

Will you be a faithful member of the Body of Christ,
and through worship and service

seek to advance God's purposes here and throughout the world?

(Candidate answers: I WILL)

After all candidates have been baptized, the congregation shall rise, and the minister shall address the congregation:

Do you promise to love, encourage, and support
these brothers and sisters
by teaching the gospel of God's love,
by being an example of Christian faith and character, and
by giving the strong support of God's family
in fellowship, prayer, and service?

(Congregation answers: WE DO)

f. The Apostles' Creed (optional)
The congregation and the candidates may join in affirming the faith in the words of the Apostles' Creed.

I believe in God, the Father almighty,
creator of heaven and earth.

I believe in Jesus Christ, his only Son, our LORD.
who was conceived by the Holy Spirit
and born of the virgin Mary.
He suffered under Pontius Pilate,
was crucified, died, and was buried;
he descended to hell.
The third day he rose again from the dead.
He ascended to heaven
and is seated at the right hand of God the Father almighty.
From there he will come to judge the living and the dead.

I believe in the Holy Spirit,
the holy universal church,
the communion of saints,
the forgiveness of sins,
the resurrection of the body,
and the life everlasting. Amen.

g. Prayer of thanksgiving

The minister says this prayer or a prayer of their own choosing:

> The LORD be with you.
> Let us give thanks to the LORD our God.
>
> We give you thanks, O holy and gracious God,
> for the gift of water.
> In the beginning your Spirit moved over the waters.
> In the waters of the flood you destroyed evil.
> You led the children of Israel through the sea
> into the freedom of the promised land.
> In the river Jordan, John baptized our LORD
> and your Spirit anointed him.
> By his death and resurrection Jesus Christ, the living water,
> frees us from sin and death and opens the way to life everlasting.
>
> We thank you, O God, for the gift of baptism.
> In this water you confirm to us
> that we are buried with Christ in his death,
> raised to share in his resurrection,
> and are being renewed by the Holy Spirit.
>
> Pour out on us your Holy Spirit,
> so that those here baptized may be washed clean and receive new life.
> To you be all honor and glory, dominion and power,
> now and forever, through Jesus Christ our LORD. Amen.

h. The baptism

The minister shall say:

> (*Name of Candidate*),
> I baptize you in the name of the Father,
> and of the Son,
> and of the Holy Spirit. Amen.

The minister will immerse the candidate in the water:

i. Prayer

The minister shall offer prayer. The following prayer may be used, or the minister may compose a unique prayer for this occasion:

> Let us pray.
>
> Gracious God,
> we thank you that you cleanse and renew
> these your children through your grace alone.
> Bless and strengthen them daily
> with the gift of your Holy Spirit;
> unfold to them the riches of your love,
> deepening their faith,
> keeping them from the power of evil,
> and enabling them to live a holy and blameless life
> until your kingdom comes.

The following blessing may be said:

> The LORD bless you and keep you;
> the LORD make his face to shine upon you,
> and be gracious to you;
> the LORD lift up his countenance upon you,
> and give you peace. Amen.

j. Close with worship

The occasion of water baptism is a wonderful event that should close with worship and praise. There is great rejoicing in heaven when a person enters the Kingdom of God (Luke 15:7). Music should be prepared for this celebration of worship.

3. Practical considerations

The opportunity for water baptism should be offered to the congregation on a regular basis. When planning a water baptism service, several practical concerns come to mind.

a. Location

The locating of a suitable body of water may be difficult in some situations. Water baptism can be accomplished in a natural body of water, such as a river or lake. If you choose such a site, you must account for the possible difficulties of entering and leaving the water. The ground can be slippery and dangerous. If using a baptistry, the water should be heated at least to room temperature to prevent the participants from contracting a chill.

b. Clothing

The candidates for baptism should be instructed regarding the best types of clothing to wear in the water. Baptismal robes are the preferred choice.

c. Towels

A sufficient number of towels should be available.

d. Music

Appropriate music should be prepared for worship before the baptism and afterwards.

C. The LORD's Supper

The most common sacrament is the LORD's Supper, also called Holy Communion, or the Eucharist. Liturgical churches celebrate the Eucharist in every worship service, but Protestant churches vary in the frequency of the rite. Because of its theological and historical importance, I would suggest having Holy Communion at least every two months.

1. The meaning of the LORD's Supper

The LORD's Supper is a sacrament that commemorates the sacrificial death of our LORD Jesus Christ. It signifies our union with him and with each other. It is our participation in his crucifixion. The LORD's Supper was commanded by Jesus as a sacramental sign that reminds us of his past deliverance, affirms his present ministry to us, and anticipates his future kingdom. The LORD's Supper should be celebrated often in the local church.

We receive our teachings on the LORD's Supper from the gospels, in which Jesus instituted the sacrament, and from the book of 1 Corinthians, in which the apostle Paul gives extended discussion of the Supper. We find the following account in the Gospel according to Luke:

> And He took bread, gave thanks and broke it, and gave it to them, saying, "This is My body which is given for you; do this in remembrance of Me." Likewise He also took the cup after supper, saying, "This cup is the new covenant in My blood, which is shed for you" (Luke 22:19-20).

The apostle Paul, in his instructions to the church at Corinth, repeats the story and adds important guidelines that believers should follow when they celebrate Communion:

> For I received from the LORD that which I also delivered to you: that the LORD Jesus on the same night in which He was betrayed took bread; and when He had given thanks, He broke it and said, "Take, eat; this is My body which is broken for you; do this in remembrance of Me." In the same manner He also took the cup after supper, saying, "This cup is the new covenant in My blood. This do, as often as you drink it, in remembrance of Me." For as often as you eat this bread and drink this cup, you proclaim the LORD's death till He comes. Therefore whoever eats this bread or drinks this cup of the LORD in an unworthy manner will be guilty of the body and blood of the LORD. But let a man examine himself, and so let him eat of the bread and drink of the cup. For he who eats and drinks in an unworthy manner eats and drinks judgment to himself, not discerning the LORD's body. For this reason many are weak and sick among you, and many sleep (1 Corinthians 11:20-34).

These biblical texts clarify the meaning of the LORD'S Supper in several ways.

a. The bread and the cup represent the body and blood of Jesus.

Before his death, Jesus had taught that his disciples must eat his flesh and drink his blood (John 6). Not understanding what Jesus meant, many disciples left him. When Jesus was sacrificed as the Passover lamb, the reference to eating his body became clear, because the Passover lamb had been eaten by the Israelites in Exodus 12.

b. The blood of Jesus is the seal of the new covenant.

Under the old covenant, sin was covered by the blood of bulls, goats, and sheep; but under the new covenant, all sin is covered by the blood of Jesus (Hebrews 9).

c. The LORD's Supper is a service of remembering Christ's death.

The grape juice and the bread do not have any power in themselves, but they remind us of the power that is found in the blood of Jesus. The LORD's Supper causes us to remember how God saved us, to remember how he delivered us, to remember how he has kept us, to remember how he has cared for us. The LORD's Supper is a reminder:

It reminds us that while we were yet sinners, Christ died for us.
It reminds us that God loved us so much that he gave his Son.
It reminds us that Jesus was wounded for our transgressions.
It reminds us that he bore our sins in his body on the cross.
It reminds us that he nailed our sins to the cross.
It reminds us that his body was broken for us.
It reminds us that by his stripes we are healed.
It reminds us that he purchased our redemption with his blood.
It reminds us that he reconciled us to God.
It reminds us that he has cleansed us from all iniquity.
It reminds us that he has purified for himself a peculiar people.
It reminds us that the crucified Christ is also our coming King.

d. The LORD's Supper is a symbol of our present relationship.

The LORD's Supper not only looks backward to the crucifixion, but it also looks at our present relationship to God and to one another. That is why Paul, in another Scripture, refers to the LORD's Supper as "Communion." He writes,

The cup of blessing which we bless, is it not the **communion** of the blood of Christ? The bread which we break, is it not the **communion** of the Body of Christ? For we, though many, are one bread and one body; for we all partake of that one bread (1 Corinthians 10:16-17).

By using the terminology of Communion, Paul emphasizes the sharing of life. Communion signifies sharing, and Holy Communion symbolizes our shared life with Christ and our shared life with other believers.

1. Communion demonstrates our union with Christ
When we gather together to eat of the LORD's Supper, as we drink the juice and as we eat the bread, each element actually becomes a part of us. The wheat and the fruit of the vine goes through a transference and is used by our bodies as energy. The essence from which it is made becomes our essence. It becomes a part of us. Similarly, as Christians, we have partaken of Jesus Christ (Hebrews 3:14). When we take of the bread and the fruit of the vine, we are testifying that we share a union with the Son of God. We are spiritually joined with him in a manner whereby we eat his flesh and drink his blood. We are in union with Christ, and our lifestyle must reflect that union.

2. Communion demonstrates our union with the Body of Christ
This communion, which signifies our fellowship in the salvation work of our Savior, also demonstrates our unity in redemption. We are all loved of God. If we have received him, he is working in all of our lives, and we all are important to God. Paul says, "For we, though many, are one bread." In Christ, we have become members of one body. In partaking of this communion, we signify our oneness and togetherness in Christ. That is why it is important that we repent of anything that would divide us as the Body of Christ, or separate us from our ministry as the Body of Christ.

We are the Body of Christ, and Communion reminds us that we are one bread. Regardless of our race; we are one bread. Regardless of our social economic status; we are one bread. Regardless of our talents and abilities; we are one bread. As the one bread of the Body of Christ, we stand in unity with each other in love. Thus, the Communion service represents our communion with God, but it also represents our communion with each other.[2]

---

[2] I acknowledge my appreciation to Rev. Robert Massey, who shared some of this material with me.

e. The LORD's Supper anticipates the soon return of our King.
When Jesus instituted the Supper, he made it clear that he would not "drink of the fruit of the vine" until the Kingdom of God had come (Matthew 26:29; Mark 14:25; Luke 22:18). Therefore, every time we partake of Communion, we are looking forward to sharing the table with Jesus Christ in the Kingdom of God. The apostle Paul stated our anticipation this way: "For as often as you eat this bread and drink this cup, you proclaim the LORD's death till He comes" (1 Corinthians 11:26). Therefore, the sacrament of the LORD's Supper is an outward visible sign of the inward spiritual grace of hope and patience. Our celebration of the LORD's Supper strengthens our hope in Christ's return and our patience as we live by faith.

f. The LORD's Supper must not be eaten carelessly.
Communion is a joyous celebration, but it is also a sobering event that recalls the LORD's crucifixion. Therefore, Paul declared that the sacredness of the Supper requires that we eat in a worthy manner. He writes,

> whoever eats this bread or drinks this cup of the LORD in an **unworthy** manner will be guilty of the body and blood of the LORD. But let a man examine himself, and so let him eat of the bread and drink of the cup. For he who eats and drinks in an **unworthy** manner eats and drinks judgment to himself, not discerning the LORD's body. For this reason many are weak and sick among you, and many sleep (1 Corinthians 11:20-34).

If we do not appreciate the sacredness of Holy Communion and if we eat insincerely, we will suffer the judgment of God. In fact, some of the people at Corinth had become sick because of their abuse of the LORD's Supper. Some had even died! To eat in a "worthy manner" means that we recognize the measureless value of the body and blood of Jesus, that we take seriously the cost of our salvation. Therefore, Paul advises that every person "examine" their hearts before partaking of Holy Communion. However, we must not be so afraid of being "unworthy" that we abstain from communion. After we examine ourselves and turn our hearts and minds to the cross, we can come joyfully to receive the grace that awaits us at the LORD's table.

3. Order of Service for the LORD's Supper

The following order of service is designed to be used when the LORD's Supper occupies the entire worship service (one hour or more). If you celebrate the LORD's Supper frequently or as part of a regular worship service, you will want to shorten the outline considerably.

a. Introduction

As we come together in the presence of the LORD to hear his Word and to partake of his table, we come as his people to celebrate our unity with him and with each other.

b. Prayer

Let us begin this Communion service in unity, reciting together the LORD's Prayer:

> Our Father who art in heaven, hallowed be thy name
> Thy Kingdom come,
> thy will be done in earth as it is in heaven,
> Give us this day our daily bread
> And forgive us our trespasses,
> as we forgive those who trespass against us.
> Lead us not into temptation, but deliver us from evil,
> For thine is the kingdom, the power, and the glory,
> forever and ever. Amen

> Now, LORD, as we draw near to you, pour out upon us the spirit of grace and of supplication. Give us warm hearts, and let our minds be fixed upon you, that we may worship you in spirit and in truth.

c. Old Testament Scripture

Choose a Scripture from those listed below at the end of this section or another that you may find relevant.

d. Worship chorus

e. New Testament Scripture

Choose a Scripture from those listed below at the end of this section or another that you may find relevant.

f. Worship chorus

g. Sermon

If you celebrate Communion infrequently, you may want to devote the entire sermon to an aspect of the LORD's Supper. However, if Communion is celebrated monthly (or weekly), you may need to address other topics, and preach on the subject of the LORD's Supper once or twice a year.

h. Prayer of examination and repentance

Use Exodus 20 or Psalm 51 as an encouragement to repentance. You may want to explain the meaning of the admonition to partake "worthily." The following is an example:

Because the LORD's Supper is a reenactment of the LORD's death, we must recognize its sacredness. If you eat and drink insincerely, and irreverently, you will face God's judgment. To eat and drink "worthily" means that we recognize the value of the body and the blood of the LORD, the importance of his death. Oh, what a blessing to share in the sufferings of our LORD. Let us pray to receive the LORD's Supper in a worshipful way.

i. Scriptural re-affirmation

Read one of the following to affirm our forgiveness: Titus 2:11-14; Titus 3:3-7; 1 Timothy 1:15; 3:16.

j. Special song

k. Scriptural account of the LORD's Supper

Read 1 Corinthians 11:17-32 or one of the gospel accounts of the LORD's Supper (Matthew 26; Mark 14; Luke 22).

l. Prayer of thanksgiving

(Call the ushers to the front if they have not already come forward).

Father, we now celebrate this memorial of our redemption.

We recall Christ's death, his descent among the dead, his glorious resurrection, and his ascension to your right hand; and, looking forward to his coming in glory, we offer unto you our praise. Let all of us be as one, who share today in the LORD's table.

Father, hear the prayers of this family gathered here before you; even before we ask you know all that we have need of, and you are the supplier of those needs.

Remember, O LORD, your church, to deliver it from all evil, and to perfect it in your love. Gather your church together, the church which you have sanctified; gather us into the Kingdom that you have prepared for us,

So that we may enjoy the vision of your glory, in the unity of the Spirit. All glory and honor is yours, Almighty Father, forever and ever, AMEN.

m. Distribution of the elements
Have a congregational or special song while distributing the bread and grape juice.

n. Administering the LORD's Supper
Bread (lift up the bread while saying the prayer)

> Prayer of Thanks:
> Blessed be the name of the LORD, Creator of all things,
> who brings forth bread from the earth.
> The body of the LORD Jesus Christ was given for us,
> that we might become part of his body.
> As we remember that Christ died for us,
> Let us partake with thanksgiving,
> And let us feed on that living bread in our hearts, by faith.
> "Take and eat, this is my body which is broken for you.
> This do in remembrance of me."
> Let us eat together (Eat the bread).

Wine (Lift up the cup while saying the prayer)

> Prayer of Thanks: "Blessed be the name of the LORD, King of the Universe, who brings forth the fruit of the vine."
>
> This is the blood that our LORD Jesus Christ shed for us,
> to purchase our redemption.
> As we remember that he died for us
> Let us partake of the Cup with thanksgiving,
> And let us drink of that living water in our hearts, by faith.

"This is the new testament in my blood which is shed for the forgiveness of sins. This do in remembrance of me."
Let us drink together (Drink the cup).

(Allow time for the people to worship the LORD and for the Holy Spirit to move. This is a good time to pray for the sick.)

o. Collecting the cups
Sing either choruses or a hymn while collecting the cups.

p. Blessing and dismissal
Now may the God of Peace,
Who brought forth from the dead our LORD Jesus Christ,
That great shepherd of the sheep,
Through the blood of the everlasting covenant,
Make you mature in every good work to do his will,
As he works in you what pleases him,
Through Jesus Christ,
To whom be glory, now and forever.
Amen.

Go in the peace of Christ
To love and serve the one, true, living God,
And to wait in hope and expectancy for the return of his son.
Amen.

4. Additional helps for conducting the LORD's Supper

a. Some suggested songs
Hymns
At the Cross
The Blood Will Never Lose its Power
What Can Wash Away My Sins
Just as I am
Amazing Grace
The Old Rugged Cross
When I See the Blood
Choruses
He Was Wounded for Our Transgressions
Oh, The Blood of Jesus

Hallelujah
Other Songs
Watch the Lamb
The LORD's Prayer
Precious Blood
I Should Have Been Crucified
Peace (A Communion Blessing), by Rich Mullins
Holiness is What I Long for

b. *Some suggested Scripture selections*
(These texts relate to the forgiveness of sins and to the meaning of
the LORD's Supper.)

Genesis 3	Genesis 22:1-14
Exodus 12	Exodus 20
Psalm 22	Isaiah 53
Matthew 22:37	Matthew 27
John 1:29	John 8:10-11
Romans 3	1 Corinthians 11:17-32
Philippians 2:5-11	Hebrews 9
Revelation 4	

Questions for Review and Application

1. Define the word "sacrament."

2. How are sacraments related to the biblical concept of "mystery"?

3. Name the five sacraments that have been suggested by Pentecostal scholars.

4. What are the sacraments that are accepted by YOUR church?

5. Explain the meaning of water baptism.

6. Why should converts be baptized?

7. List three Scriptures that teach water baptism.

8. Write out a brief statement to the congregation that you could use when conducting a water baptism service.

9. Name four practical considerations when planning a water baptism service.

10. What is the most common sacrament?

11. Explain the meaning of the Lord's Supper.

12. How does the Lord's Supper relate to the past, the present, and the future?

13. What is the significance of the term "Communion"?

14. Explain Paul's command that we should not eat "unworthily."

15. Read Exodus 12, and name three ways that it relates to the Lord's Supper.

16. Besides the songs listed in the book, suggest three other songs that would be appropriate for use during the Lord's Supper.

~⊙ CHAPTER 10 ⊙~

SACRAMENTS AND CEREMONIES (PART 2)

If I then, your LORD and Teacher, have washed your feet, you also ought to wash one another's feet (John 13:14).

This chapter continues the discussion of the sacraments and other ceremonies that occur in the context of a worship service. We will discuss footwashing, prayer for the sick, and the dedication of children.

A. Footwashing

Footwashing is perhaps the most misunderstood and unappreciated of the sacramental signs. Most people are not aware that footwashing is accepted as a valid practice in most of the world's churches. It is practiced annually (usually during Holy Week) in eastern Orthodox churches, Anglican churches, Roman Catholic churches, and many major Protestant denominations.

1. The meaning of footwashing

For Pentecostals, footwashing is the outward visible sign of the inward work of sanctification. In biblical times, the washing of feet was an act of hospitality that was normally performed for guests by a servant or by the wife of the host. In John's gospel, Jesus washed his disciples' feet during the meal that we call the Last Supper. The LORD instituted the footwashing sacrament in the following manner:

> Jesus, knowing that the Father had given all things into His hands, and that He had come from God and was going to God, rose from supper and laid aside His garments, took a towel and

girded Himself. After that, He poured water into a basin and began to wash the disciples' feet, and to wipe them with the towel with which He was girded. Then He came to Simon Peter. And Peter said to Him, "LORD, are You washing my feet?" Jesus answered and said to him, "What I am doing you do not understand now, but you will know after this." Peter said to Him, "You shall never wash my feet!" Jesus answered him, "If I do not wash you, you have no part with Me." Simon Peter said to Him, "LORD, not my feet only, but also my hands and my head!" Jesus said to him, "He who is bathed needs only to wash his feet, but is completely clean; and you are clean, but not all of you." For He knew who would betray Him; therefore He said, "You are not all clean." So when He had washed their feet, taken His garments, and sat down again, He said to them, "Do you know what I have done to you? You call me Teacher and LORD, and you say well, for so I am. If I then, your LORD and Teacher, have washed your feet, you also ought to wash one another's feet. For I have given you an example, that you should do as I have done to you. Most assuredly, I say to you, a servant is not greater than his master; nor is he who is sent greater than he who sent him. If you know these things, blessed are you if you do them" (John 13:3-17).

The washing of feet continued in the early Christian church. The requirements for enrollment on the list of widows includes the expectation that a widow would have "washed the saints' feet" (1 Timothy 5:10).

There are at least five important points that we can learn from John 13. First, it was Jesus who washed the disciples' feet, and not vice versa. Second, the reason that Jesus performed the washing is explained by the purpose of the washing. Jesus washed their feet in order to make them clean. Peter asked Jesus to wash his whole body, but Jesus replied that Peter did not need his whole body to be washed because he had already taken a bath. However, on his way to the supper, Peter's feet had picked up dirt and dust from the streets. Therefore, only his feet needed cleansing. Third, this cleansing, therefore, is a picture of Jesus' ministry of cleansing after we have been baptized. Our initial salvation and cleansing from sin is represented by water baptism. However, after baptism, we walk in this world and pick up the dirt and dust along the way. Thus, we need further cleansing, which we call sanctification. We need to be baptized only once, but we need our feet washed on a regular basis The fourth point that we learn from this text is that Jesus wants us to continue the practice of footwashing. Twice he states that we should follow his example. He says, "If I then, your LORD and Teacher, have washed your feet, you also ought to wash one another's feet." Then, he restates his point: "I have given you an example, that you should do as I have done to you." Fifth, the practice of footwashing is accompanied by God's blessing. Jesus completes his explanation of footwashing by saying, "If you know these things, blessed are you if you do them."

When we wash someone's feet, we are taking on the ministry of Jesus to offer cleansing and forgiveness. After the resurrection, Jesus authorized his disciples to fulfill the ministry of forgiveness. Jesus said to them, "If you forgive the sins of any, they are forgiven them" (John 20:23). We serve one another by sanctifying one another.

When we submit to having our feet washed, we are admitting our need for continued cleansing. In having our feet washed, we are sanctified and cleansed "with the washing of water by the word" (Ephesians 5:26; see also John 17:17). We are surrendering to the sanctifying effect of the blood of Jesus (Hebrews 13:12) through the power of the Holy Spirit (1 Peter 1:2).

2. The footwashing service

The following outline or a variation of it may be used in a footwashing service.

a. Song

It is always appropriate to begin with a song. Encourage everyone to worship. Music should be prepared to be played in the background throughout the footwashing service.

b. Introductory comments

The washing of one another's feet, following the example of Jesus when he washed the feet of his disciples, is a symbol of our need for renewed cleansing and forgiveness, made possible by the love of God and the grace of the LORD Jesus Christ. By kneeling and washing, we fulfill Jesus' ministry of forgiveness and sanctification. By having our feet washed, we confess our need for continual cleansing by the blood of Christ, by the Word of God, and through the Holy Spirit.

c. Scripture reading

The leader says, "Hear the Word of the LORD from John 13."

Read John 13:1–17.

d. Prayer

The leader or someone assigned should offer a prayer. The following is an example:

> LORD God, we praise you and give you thanks, because you laid aside your power as a garment and took upon yourself the form of a slave. You became obedient unto death, even death on a cross. Come now, Holy Spirit, wash us and make us one body in Christ; that, as we are bound together in this gesture of love, we may no longer be in bondage to the principalities and powers that enslave creation, but may know your liberating peace such as the world cannot give. Amen.

e. The footwashing

The footwashing may begin with a brief announcement of procedure – where basins and towels are located, how persons should pair up, or a request that participants return to their seats following the washing.

Depending upon how the chairs are arranged, footwear may be removed at the pews or near the water basins.

Footwashing should be done in pairs. One person will sit while another kneels before the basin. The two persons should pray for one another and worship as the footwashing proceeds. The person kneeling should wrap themselves with a towel, then lift one of the person's feet into the basin. After washing the foot, they will then lift and dry it. The process is repeated with the other foot. Then, the two persons switch position, and the washer has their feet washed.

Men should wash the feet of men, and women should wash the feet of women.

Participants then replace their footwear and return to their seats where they continue to worship and pray.

f. Worship
Music and worship should continue as people are finishing up and reassembling.

g. Closing prayer
The leader or someone appointed may offer a closing prayer, or the group may pray in unison as the Spirit leads.

3. Practical considerations
Everyone should be instructed to come to the service with clean feet. This is a ritual and does not require soap or scrubbing.

Women should be reminded not to wear stockings or pantyhose, which would be difficult to remove.

Prepare a sufficient number of bowls and towels.

When choosing the location of the footwashing, consider the fact that water will get on the floor.

Have the bowls filled with warm water before the service begins.

The men and women should be separated into different rooms or different areas of the sanctuary.

B. Prayer for the sick and anointing with oil

Prayer for the sick and anointing with oil should be an important part of every worship service. Jesus healed the sick during the Jewish worship services in the synagogue (Matthew 12:9-13; Mark 1:21-26). Peter and John healed a lame man when they went to the temple for prayer services (Acts 3:1-8). The Gospel of Mark tells us that we should "lay hands on the sick, and they will recover" (Mark 16:18); and James gives instructions that we should follow when praying for the sick (James 5:14-16).

1. The meaning of anointing with oil

The anointing oil represents the Holy Spirit, and anointing with oil is a sign of divine healing. We believe that Jesus died that we might live. He purchased our complete redemption on the cross. Isaiah spoke about the power of Christ's sacrificial death:

> But He was wounded for our transgressions,
>   He was bruised for our iniquities;
> The chastisement for our peace was upon Him,
>   And by His stripes we are healed" (Isaiah 53:5).

The redemption purchased by Christ includes the healing of the human body which was affected by the fall. As a sign of our complete healing (a spiritual body), God now heals the sick. Jesus came to deliver from the consequences of sin, and those consequences include disease. God heals because he loves. God heals as a sign of the kingdom. God heals because it brings glory to his name. God heals as a confirmation of his word.

The apostle James provides instructions for the Church regarding anointing with oil. He writes,

> Is anyone among you suffering? Let him pray. Is anyone cheerful? Let him sing psalms. Is anyone among you sick? Let him call for the elders of the church, and let them pray over him, **anointing** him with oil in the name of the LORD. And the prayer of faith will save the sick, and the LORD will raise him up. And if he has committed sins, he will be forgiven. Confess your trespasses to one another, and pray for one another, that you may be healed. The effective, fervent prayer of a righteous man avails much (James 5:13-16).

James' instructions reveal a number of important aspects of the church's role in praying for the sick. First, prayer for the sick occurs within the overall context of worship. James mentions prayer, singing, forgiveness, and confession. All of these together suggest the context of a worship service. Second, the prayer should be accompanied by anointing with oil. There is not power in the oil, but the oil represents the Holy Spirit. Third, the prayer and the anointing should be done by the elders of the church. All believers should pray for the sick (Mark 16:18), but the elders should take the lead and serve as examples and teachers to everyone else. Fourth, those who pray must pray in faith. James does not say that the sick person must have faith, although it is all the better if they do. Fifth, it is the LORD who heals; we do not heal. Our role is to pray and to anoint; God's role is to heal. Sixth, sins will be forgiven. Although we should never blame the sufferer for their illness, it is always possible that they are hindered in their faith by the presence of unforgiven sin. We should encourage the sick person to confess any sin that the Holy Spirit brings to their mind.

2. Order of service for anointing with oil

As long as we follow James' instructions and the leading of the Holy Spirit, we are free to arrange the time of prayer for the sick. Some churches have a customary time for praying for the sick, and others vary the time from week to week. I would suggest that prayer for the sick be placed on the program or order of service every week. The following outline can be followed when praying for the sick.

a. A Leader states that the time has come to pray for the sick. You may also want to pray for other needs at the same time.

b. Reading of Scripture.

Some suggested Scriptures are Exodus 15:26; Psalm 103:1-3; Isaiah 53:4-5; Malachi 4:2; Matthew 4:23; 8:17; Mark 16:18; Luke 4:18; Acts 3:1-8; 10:38; Hebrews 13:8; 1 Peter 2:24; and James 5:13-16.

c. Brief explanation of our teaching on divine healing and anointing with oil.

If you have newcomers in the worship service, they may not be aware of the Pentecostal beliefs regarding divine healing. A brief teaching is always in order. You may use the following as an example:

Many of our friends and loved ones are suffering. They are enduring the pain of sickness and disease. Ever since Adam and Eve sinned in the Garden of Eden, sickness has been a part of the human experience. From birth to death, sickness is close at hand.

God, however, has given us good news. He is our healer. In Exodus 15:26, God told Israel, "I am the LORD who heals you." It is God's nature to heal. As soon as the curse of sin brought sickness into this world, God began to fulfill his plan of redemption. That plan includes the eradication of all sickness from the earth. God promised through the prophet Malachi, "The Sun of Righteousness shall arise with healing in His wings" (4:2). God healed in Israel in the Bible days. God healed during the ministry of Jesus. God healed through the Apostles. God has continued to heal throughout history. In recent times, God has renewed our belief in divine healing as he worked through men and women of God to heal all manner of sickness and disease. God is still the healer.

To begin his ministry, Jesus chose a passage from the book of Isaiah that says, "The Spirit of the LORD is upon Me, because He has anointed Me ... to heal the brokenhearted" (Luke 4.18). Healing was a major characteristic of Jesus' public ministry. According to Matthew 4:23, "Jesus went about all Galilee, teaching in their synagogues, preaching the gospel of the kingdom, and healing all kinds of sickness and all kinds of disease among the people" (Matthew 4:23). And "He Himself took our infirmities and bore our sicknesses" (Matthew 8:17). Jesus' healing ministry fulfills the prophecy of Isaiah, who said,

> He was wounded for our transgressions,
>> He was bruised for our iniquities;
> The chastisement for our peace was upon Him,
>> And by His stripes we are healed (Isaiah 53:5).

Peter, an eyewitness of Jesus' ministry says that Jesus "went about doing good and healing all who were oppressed by the devil" (Acts 10:38). Jesus himself said that he did the works of his Heavenly Father (John 10:37). God is our healer.

From Genesis to Revelation, God is healer. In the end, there will be no more sickness, no more pain, no more death. We will all eat freely from the tree of life, the tree of healing (Revelation 21:4; 2:7).

d. Gather the sick at the altar.

You should have a list of names that you can share with the Church before you pray. Some of the sick people will not be able to attend the worship service, and you can send them an anointed cloth (See Acts 19:11-12). You can feel free to pray for other needs as well.

e. Call for the elders to come to the altar.

This step may also be done at the very beginning. You should have several vials of anointing oil so that each elder will have access to the oil.

f. Anoint each person and pray for their healing.

You may want to conclude with praise and thanksgiving or with testimonies of anyone who was healed.

3. Anointed prayer cloths

From the beginning of the movement, Pentecostal churches have used anointed prayer cloths as a means of ministering healing to the sick. Whenever a sick person was unable (or unwilling) to attend the worship service, a family member or friend would ask for a prayer cloth that would be sent to the suffering person. They would place the cloth on the affected area and pray for healing.

The practice is based upon the experience of the apostle Paul. Luke reports that as Paul ministered in Ephesus and throughout Asia Minor, the following events transpired: "Now God worked unusual miracles by the hands of Paul, so that even handkerchiefs or aprons were brought from his body to the sick, and the diseases left them and the evil spirits went out of them" (Acts 19:11-12). The handkerchiefs had no power in themselves. They were not magic. However, they pointed to the healer, Jesus, and served as physical signs of the power of the Holy Spirit.

Paul's experience is not that strange if we consider that a woman was healed by touching Jesus' clothing (Luke 8:44; see also Matthew 13:46), and others looked for healing in Peter's shadow (Acts 5:15). In the Old Testament, Naaman was healed of leprosy when he dipped seven times in the Jordan River (2 Kings 5:14), and a man was raised from the dead when he fell upon the bones of Elisha (2 Kings 13:21).

Early Pentecostals prayed over anointed cloths on a regular basis, normally during the time of the service when they prayed for the sick. Prayer cloths are an extension of the Church's ministry of healing. When the congregation is unable to "lay hands on the sick" (Mark 16:18), they can lay hands on an anointed cloth and send it to the person who is suffering. The sick person should be told to look to Jesus for healing as they take courage through the anointed cloth, which represents the prayers of the believers.[1]

C. The dedication of children

1. The reason for the child dedication ceremony

Children are a gift of God, and the birth of a child is cause for celebration. Every child is valuable to God and should be cared for in the Body of Christ. The ceremony of dedicating a child to the LORD is a way for parents to express their thanksgiving to God and to make a commitment to bring up the Child in the nurture and admonition of the LORD. The dedication of children is not a sacrament, but I include it here because of its importance as a ceremony within the context of worship.

The tradition of dedicating children to the LORD has a long and rich history in the Bible. The Law of Moses required that the first child born in a family should be dedicated on its eighth day. We read in the book of 1 Samuel that Hannah dedicated her son Samuel to the LORD. In the New Testament, Mary and Joseph brought their baby Jesus to the temple in Jerusalem in order to present him before the LORD. In the same way, parents today bring their children to the House of God and dedicate them to God.

The dedication of a child to the LORD does not make that child a Christian. The child must make that decision for themselves when they are old enough to do so. However, all children are kept by God's saving grace until they reach the age of accountability.

---

[1] For a more complete study of the use of prayer cloths, see Thomas, "Toward a Pentecostal Theology of Anointed Cloths," in Lee Roy Martin (ed.), *Toward a Pentecostal Theology of Worship* (Cleveland, TN: CPT Press, 2016), pp. 91-113.

A Ceremony of Child Dedication is an opportunity for the parents (1) to give thanks for the child that God has given them, (2) to surrender their child to the will of God, and (3) to dedicate themselves to the training of the child in the Word of God and the Christian faith.

Scriptures that may be used in dedicating children include Deuteronomy 6:4-7; Psalm 127:3; Proverbs 22:6; 1 Samuel 1:27-28; Psalm 78:4-7; Ephesians 6:1-4; Luke 2:22-23; Ephesians 6:4.

2. Suggested guidelines for participation

Parents who desire to dedicate their child should meet certain minimal qualifications.

a. The parents should be living a Christian life, participating in the church.

b. The parents should present the child before age six.

c. An unwed parent should talk to the pastor about their situation.

d. Someone other than the parents can dedicate the child if they have legal guardianship.

3. Ceremony of Child Dedication

You may use this Child Dedication ceremony in its entirety, or you can modify it to suit your own context and needs.

a. Introduction

Today we will dedicate *a child/children* to the LORD. Along with the families, we bring *him/her/them* to the LORD for dedication. In the book of Judges, the LORD tells us about the tragedy of a generation that lost touch with God. Judges 2:10 says, "another generation arose after them who did not know the LORD nor the work which He had done for Israel." We owe it to our children to raise them in the nurture and the admonition of the LORD.

(Call for the parents, the child, and any family members to come forward and face the minister.)

Address the parents:

Parents Names, life is a stewardship. It is not your own; you have been bought with a price – the precious blood of God's own Son. Life is, therefore, God's gift to you. It is to be returned to him fulfilled and glorifying to him. The opportunities and experiences in life are experiences in stewardship and worship. We are charged to render each experience to God.

Marriage is a stewardship in which one man and one woman are joined by God to be one flesh. Marriage is returned to God as an act of divine worship when two people live their lives in such a way that they embody the relationship between Christ and the church.

Parenthood is a stewardship. This child which we will dedicate today is not your own; *he/she* belongs to God. God gave *his/her* life and that life will be returned to God. You are the keepers of this treasure.

You are the developers of this treasure. You are answerable to God for the manner in which you keep and develop this treasure.

God has given you a privilege. You have the opportunity to return to God a treasure developed to its full potential spiritually and socially.

This stewardship requires certain commitments on your part. You are not prepared to dedicate this child unless you are yourself dedicated to Christ as your Savior and LORD.

You are not prepared to believe for this child unless you believe for yourself and for your salvation. Although your faith will be no substitute for this child's personal faith, it is essential to your act of dedication and to your stewardship.

b. *Pledges of Dedication*
I will ask you in Christ's Name to affirm or to reaffirm your personal faith in Jesus Christ as your Savior and LORD.

To the father: *Father's Name*, do you now affirm that Jesus Christ is your Savior and LORD? (Response: I do.)

To the mother: *Mother's Name*, do you now affirm that Jesus Christ is your Savior and LORD?

(Response: I do.)

I now address the other family members along with the parents.

Please respond to the following pledges of dedication with the words, "*We Dedicate Ourselves.*"

To live a life of personal faith in Jesus Christ
We Dedicate Ourselves

To exemplify in the home the grace of God
We Dedicate Ourselves

To live by the love of God demonstrated in thought, word, and deed
We Dedicate Ourselves

To raise this child in the nurture and admonition of the LORD
We Dedicate Ourselves

To instill in this child a love for the Word of God and faithfulness in the worship of God
We Dedicate Ourselves

   c. Congregational Covenant
Will the congregation please stand and share in this act of dedication.

With the birth and dedication of *Child's Name*, this congregation has also inherited a stewardship. These parents standing alone are not sufficient to the vows which they have just taken. This child on his own will not come to know Jesus Christ as Savior and LORD.

These vows and the goal of personal salvation can be realized only in a community of faith. You, as the congregation of God, are charged by God to provide a nurturing and supporting community of spiritual oversight and nurture for this child and his parents.

Please respond in unison to the following pledges with the words, "*We Dedicate Ourselves:*"

To provide for *Child's Name* a household of faith – the temple of the Holy Spirit
We Dedicate Ourselves

To provide for *Child's Name* a sanctuary of prayer and love
  We Dedicate Ourselves

To pray for *Parent's Names* in the fulfillment of the vows which
they have taken before God
  We Dedicate Ourselves

To pray for *Child's Name* that *he/she* will come to an experience
of saving faith early in life
  We Dedicate Ourselves

To follow *Child's Name* with our prayers and love throughout
his/her life.
  We Dedicate Ourselves

  d. Presentation of Bible
Parent's Names, I present you with this Bible for *Child's Name*.
This is God's Word. It is God's Word for *him/her*.
It is a lamp unto *his/her* feet and a light unto *his/her* path (Psalm
119:105).
It will guide *him/her* into paths of righteousness (Psalm 23:3).
It is able to make *him/her* wise unto salvation (2 Timothy 3:15).
It will strengthen *him/her* against temptation (Psalm 119:9).
It will heal *his/her* sicknesses (Psalm 107:20).
It is a mirror of the soul (James 1:23).
It is a mighty sword (Ephesians 6:17).
It is sweeter than honey and more precious than gold (Psalm
19:10).

  e. Prayer of dedication
(The minister should receive the child from the parents and offer
this prayer of dedication, or another prayer as the Spirit leads.)

To you, our heavenly Father,
  the Author of life,

To you, our LORD Jesus,
  the Light who Lights everyone coming into the world,

To you, Holy Spirit, the Breath of life,

To God, Three in One, Oh, glorious Trinity we come.

We come in covenant with you
a covenant which we have received in grace.

We thank you for this child, *Child's Name*, your gift to us and to this congregation and the manifestation of your life in the world.

We thank you that you have placed this child in our care.

He/she is yours, and as stewards we offer *him/her* to you.

We Dedicate Ourselves to you for the fulfillment of this covenant.

Now in faith we dedicate *Child's Name*
for the manifestation of your grace and glory.

We ask for wisdom from your Word,
for the graciousness of your love,
for the abounding of Christ's grace
and the communion of the Holy Spirit
in the fulfillment of this task.

In the Name of our LORD Jesus Christ we pray Amen.[2]

4. A covenant to nurture our children

The following covenant is suitable for printing in the church bulletin or on a certificate presented to the parents.[3]

We as parents, members, and pastors of *Church Name* covenant together to disciple our children as followers of Jesus Christ and to lead them into the church as full participants and future guardians of the Pentecostal faith and experience. We covenant to do this by drawing our children into the activities essential to the nature of the church through which the Christian faith is experienced. In order to fulfill this covenant we shall:

1. Join together in the act of dedicating our children to the LORD and communicating to them a sense of acceptance and belonging within the family of God, teaching them the lordship of Christ.

---

[2] I am indebted to Dr. R. Hollis Gause for many of the ideas in this Ceremony of Child Dedication.

[3] See John Kie Vining (ed.), *Developing Pentecostal Teens: A Covenant to Nurture Our Children* (Cleveland, TN: Pathway Press, 2 edn, 1995).

2. Prepare our children for the acts of grace uplifted by the Pentecostal faith: salvation, sanctification, and the baptism in the Holy Spirit.

3. Pray for our children daily and lead them into developing a personal prayer life.

4. Involve our children in interacting with the Bible so that the study of Scripture becomes for them an ongoing process of interpreting life from God's perspective.

5. Build nurturing relationships between our children and members of our church so that the process of modeling and mentoring in Christian living may occur.

6. Involve our children in the exercise of choice, so that personal commitments to the lifestyle of Christ and the Pentecostal faith can be made.

7. Affirm that our children have a God-given potential to minister in special ways to the church and encourage them to be so used by God in sharing their faith.

8. Prepare our children for the covenants of the Pentecostal faith: water baptism, communion and footwashing, church membership, marriage, and baby dedication.

9. Encourage our children to witness of their faith in Christ by word and by lifestyle.

Questions for Review and Application

1. Explain the sacramental significance of footwashing.

2. Write out 1 Timothy 5:10.

3. List the five important points that we can learn from John 13.

   (1)

   (2)

   (3)

   (4)

(5)

4. When we submit to footwashing, what are we confessing?

5. Prepare a short statement on the meaning of footwashing that you can use to introduce a footwashing service.

6. List three practical considerations when planning a footwashing service.

7. Write out James 5:14-16.

8. Explain the meaning of anointing with oil.

9. List six things that we learn from James 5:14-16.

   (1)

   (2)

   (3)

   (4)

   (5)

   (6)

10. Why should we pray for the sick in every service?

11. Write out Acts 19:11-12.

12. Explain the function of the anointed prayer cloth.

13. Why should we dedicate children to the Lord?

14. In addition to the guidelines listed in the book, can you think of any other guidelines for the dedication of children?

CHAPTER 11

THE POWER OF TRUE WORSHIP

Therefore if the whole church comes together in one place ... and an unbeliever or an uninformed person comes in, he is convinced by all ... and so, falling down on his face, he will worship God and report that God is truly among you (1 Corinthians 14:23-25).

A. The impact of worship on the world

1. The world watches our worship

When we talk about the Church's impact on the world, we normally emphasize evangelism and community service. Although it is true that our greatest influence is through these two ministries, there is a third area that also impacts the world – that is our worship. The world is watching our lifestyle of worship; the world sees our attitude of worship; and the world notices our acts of worship. The worship service is where Christians offer their prayers and praises to God, but their acts of worship have an effect on the community outside the four walls of the church.

The psalmist realized that just as his salvation resulted in worship, his worship produced a witness. Consider the following psalm:

He also brought me up out of a horrible pit,
    Out of the miry clay,
And set my feet upon a rock,
    And established my steps.

He has put a new song in my mouth –
    Praise to our God;
Many will see it and fear,
    And will trust in the LORD (Psalm 40:2-3).

The psalmist praises God for deliverance from the horrible pit. As he sings praises to God, many people will hear his song, and his song will cause them to fear God and to trust in God. Our worship is a witness.

On the Day of Pentecost, the 120 disciples were all filled with the Holy Spirit, and they began to praise God in other tongues. The crowd that had gathered for the feast heard the disciples praising God and uttering the "wonderful works of God" (Acts 2:11). Peter arose and preached the gospel, and 3000 souls were saved. The evangelistic preaching of Peter was preceded by Spirit-filled worship.

2. Worship as a witness

In order to impact the world, our worship should display the following characteristics:

a. We are light

Our worship should be a bright display of God's love. As we sing, as we praise God, as we pray, as we fellowship, as we testify, and as we enjoy the sacraments, unbelievers will hear of God's great love.

We are now living in a time when most people do not know the content of the Bible or the language of the Bible. They may never have heard of the golden calf or Elijah's prayer on Mt. Carmel. They may not know Zechariah, Malachi, or Jude. They may have no idea what we mean when we talk about sanctification, redemption, justification, or the Christian's armor. In order to be light, we must be clear in our manner of communicating the Word of God and the Christian faith. We must explain God's Word by using simple and direct language that people can understand. As we preach, teach, and testify, we must never assume that people already know the Bible or biblical terminology. We should be light in the darkness.

b. We are salt

Our worship should demonstrate that Christians have been changed. Non-Christians should see in our worship that we are different from people who do not know Christ. If we display genuine Christianity, the non-Christians will desire to be changed.

c. We are free

Our worship should display the joy that comes with freedom from sin and condemnation. Have you ever been to a church where everyone was sad all the time? They come in the door with a frown on their faces? They sit on the pew, and they look at their watches, and it seems as if they are in a hurry to get home. This is not the kind of worship that pleases God. We need to understand that our worship is a witness. We must demonstrate the joy of the LORD. We need to accept the personal responsibility to display the joy of the LORD. Our worship is a witness to those that are lost.

d. We are inviting

We must make time in our worship to invite unbelievers to accept the gospel. If we conduct our worship in a way that honors and glorifies God, our worship will invite the world to come to Christ. The brightness of God's love and the joy of Christian praise will be attractive to unbelievers. They will be drawn by the Holy Spirit to respond to the invitation of the gospel. The altar call is the most common way to bring sinners to repentance, but other methods can be used also. We can be creative in our methods, but we must always find a way to invite sinners to come to the cross.

Worship is the Church's most important activity in this world. It is in worship that we glorify God, strengthen the Church, and impact the world. We must take great care to conduct our worship so that we may be a positive witness for Christ.

B. The evaluation our worship

1. Questions for evaluation

If we desire to have an impact on the world, then we should evaluate our worship. Every element of worship should be examined in light of the following questions:

- Is it Biblical?
- Does it glorify God?
- What are the biblical foundations of this practice?
- Does it help form people in the faith?
- Does it minister to people's needs?
- Does it advance the purposes of the church?
- Does it cause us to love one another more?
- Does it communicate the gospel to the world?
- Does it help build unity in the Body of Christ?
- Does it enable us to worship Christ more deeply?
- Does it facilitate the moving of the Holy Spirit?
- Does it make us better witnesses?

2. Results of evaluation

An honest evaluation will reveal much helpful information regarding our worship. The information gained in the evaluation will enable us to divide our worship practices into three categories:

a. Aspects of our worship that need improvement

We should make a list of areas that are important components of worship, but in which our performance is lacking. We may need to improve our method of greeting new people, receiving the offering, sharing prayer requests, or praying in the altar. We may need to revise our music or our teaching methods.

b. Aspects of our worship that should be discarded

We may discover that some parts of our worship are no longer effective and should be abandoned completely. We should be able to explain the purpose and benefit of everything that we do in worship.

c. Aspects of our worship that we do well

While the results of evaluation usually focus on areas that need to be changed, we should not overlook the areas that we do well. Evaluation should lead not only to correction but also to celebration. We should give thanks to God for the aspects of our worship that are beneficial and inspiring. We should always take time to rejoice over the things good.

C. The believer's responsibility to worship

1. The corporate nature of worship

In many churches, the priest, the pastor, the minister, and the worship leader take full responsibility for the success or failure of the service. In these churches, the congregation has no responsibility except to do as they are told, to follow the ritual, the liturgy. When the leader tells them to pray, they pray. When the leader tells them to stand, they stand. When the leader tells them to kneel, they kneel. In the Pentecostal church, however, the congregation is an active participant, not only in the acting out of the liturgy but in the creation of the liturgy itself. If the church is the Body of Christ, and God has put his gifts in the church (1 Corinthians 12), then every member of the body has a responsibility in the worship service.

2. Preparation for worship

Every worshiper has the responsibility to prepare for worship. They should arise early enough so that they are not rushed in coming to church. They should take time to pray and to meditate on the LORD before church. They should prepare their tithe and offering. They should enter the sanctuary ready to praise God.

3. Participation in worship

a. Accepting responsibility to worship

Every worshiper must accept the responsibility to praise and worship God for themselves. "Let everything that has breath praise the LORD" (Psalm 150:6). As worshipers, we must invest ourselves in the service. We must put forth some effort to praise God and participate in the service. Every worshiper must see it as their responsibility to make the service a success.

b. Taking the initiative to worship

We have a responsibility to praise and worship God without waiting for someone to prompt us and prod us. God is looking for worshipers, and we must be spontaneous worshipers. We must not wait for the pastor or the worship leader to awaken us from the dead. We have a responsibility to enter into the worship enthusiastically and quickly. That is, we must not wait until halfway through the service before we begin to worship. The worship time is not very long, and it is a very precious time, a valuable time. We must not waste that time by procrastinating and by waiting on someone else to start worshiping. When we enter the doors of the church, we should be ready to worship!

c. Avoiding distractions in worship

It is our responsibility to avoid distractions in worship. Sometimes we blame other people for our failure to praise God. We may blame the pastor, the worship leader, the musicians, or the praise team; but if we do not praise God, it is no one's fault but our own. We must not allow anything to distract us from worshiping God!

D. Pentecostal worship

1. Pentecostal identity

Worship is at the heart of our Pentecostal identity. If Pentecostalism is to continue as a vibrant movement of the Holy Spirit, it must transmit the heart of the movement to the next generation. When I speak of the heart of the movement, I mean more than statements of doctrine; because Pentecostalism is more than just a list of certain beliefs. Our beliefs and practices combine to form a distinct spirituality. For example, the theological heart of Pentecostalism is the Fivefold Gospel – Jesus is savior, sanctifier, Spirit baptizer, healer, and soon-coming king. However, the Fivefold Gospel is more than a statement of belief; it is a way of being in the world; it is a spirituality. Spirituality, however, is not a static attainment. It must be nurtured, developed, instilled, and made steadfast by means of spiritual practices. For Pentecostalism, these spiritual practices include uninhibited worship, tarrying in prayer, seasons of fasting, caring for one another, bearing witness to the world, self-sacrifice, preaching the whole Gospel, healing the sick, immersion in God's Word, and seeking for the Spirit's gifts. All of these are done with a sense of urgency and longing in light of the soon return of Jesus. Worship is at the center of our spirituality and our experience of God, and if we make our worship to be just like that of everyone else, then we will cease to be Pentecostal. The manner in which we worship affects our way of life, our desires, our goals, and our beliefs.

2. Pentecostal experience

Furthermore, Pentecostal worship is an experience of God's grace, of which the believer testifies, "I thank God that I am saved, sanctified, filled with the Holy Ghost, trusting God with my body, and looking for Jesus to come." Therefore, if we fail to experience the Full Gospel in our worship services, we will have only "a form of godliness, but denying its power" (2 Timothy 3:5). To make this happen, pastors and other leaders must be more than administrators and "coaches;" they must be "examples to the flock" (1 Peter 5:3). They must be active participants in the pursuit of God, models of Pentecostal spirituality. Furthermore, the churches must provide continuing opportunities for people to experience salvation, sanctification, healing, and Spirit baptism. In the context of worship, our faith is strengthened, our beliefs are established, and our spiritual life is formed.

Many Pentecostal churches have eliminated revival services, and they have limited themselves to only one worship service per week, making it very difficult for seekers to find a time, a place, and communal support for extended prayer. Therefore, creative solutions that are appropriate to each context must be invented in order to provide the opportunities necessary for spiritual growth. Those who have lost their way and are bound by sin need Jesus the savior. Those who are fighting hopelessly against addictions and are harboring deep struggles need Jesus the sanctifier. Those who desire to serve God in fullness need Jesus the Spirit baptizer. Those who suffer from illnesses or emotional wounds, whether small or great, need Jesus the healer. Those who find themselves acclimating to this world order and those who find themselves as aliens in this world need Jesus the soon-coming King. God is at work, redeeming the world unto himself, and God has used the Pentecostal movement in that redemptive process.

3. Pentecostal future

Worship is only one component of Pentecostal spiritual life, but it is a vital component. If we abandon Pentecostal worship, we will cease to be Pentecostals. In many places, Pentecostal worship has been influenced by contemporary evangelical currents, including the so-called seeker-friendly, emergent, and missional models, which have pushed Pentecostalism closer in worship practices to mainline Protestantism. Unfortunately, if Pentecostalism loses the distinctive heart of its worship practices, it will also lose its distinctive spirituality, theology, and identity. Furthermore, history demonstrates that the growth of the Pentecostal church is linked to its depth of worship. Hopefully, studies like this one will help to strengthen the movement. May Pentecostals continue to affirm with the Psalmist:

> As the deer pants for brooks of water,
> So pants my soul for you, O God.
> My soul thirsts for God,
> for the living God ... (Psalm 42:2-3).

Questions for Review and Application

1. Read 1 Corinthians 14:23-25. What does it say about the impact of our worship upon unbelievers?

2. Explain how Psalm 40:1-3 shows the impact of worship on the world.

3. Describe how the disciples' worship on the Day of Pentecost resulted in 3000 souls being saved.

4. Name and explain the four characteristics of worship that help us to impact the world.

   (1)

   (2)

   (3)

   (4)

5. In addition to the twelve questions that are listed in this chapter, can you think of any other questions that would help us evaluate the effectiveness of our worship?

6. After evaluation, we should divide our worship practices into three categories. Name and explain those three categories.

(1)

(2)

(3)

7. How does the corporate nature of worship require each person to participate?

8. What should we do to prepare ourselves for worship?

9. Name and explain the three elements of participation in worship.

(1)

(2)

(3)

10. How does worship contribute to Pentecostal identity?

11. Explain how worship provides the context for Pentecostal spiritual experiences.

12. What effect will our worship have on the future of the Pentecostal movement?

CHAPTER 12

PLANNING AND PREPARING FOR WORSHIP

Whenever you come together, each of you has a psalm, has a teaching, has a tongue, has a revelation, has an interpretation. Let all things be done for edification (1 Corinthians 14:26).

In order to prepare for a successful and effective worship service, we must practice the presence of God throughout the week. Worship must be a lifestyle for us. When we learn to worship God every day, it will not be difficult to worship God on Sundays. In the same way that the psalmist declares, "I will dwell in the house of the LORD forever" (Psalm 23:6), so also we must dwell in the presence of the LORD every day if we expect to be ready to lead worship on in the House of God.

In planning a worship service, we first must recognize that anything that happens in that service is considered an opportunity for worship. Whether it is receiving the offering or the delivery of the message, whether it is the music or even the announcements, each element of the service should be done in such a way that we are directing people's attention to Jesus in adoration and thanksgiving.

A. The role of the senior pastor

With that said, let us first talk about the role of the senior pastor in the planning of a worship service. (Some pastors prefer the term "lead pastor" instead of "senior pastor" because the lead pastor may not be the oldest person on the pastoral staff.)

There are many best-case scenarios we could mention, but the truth is that the only full-time staff member in many churches is the senior pastor. Even then, many of those pastors are bi-vocational. In this scenario, there is not a lot of time for meetings; and, in this situation, the pastor has very limited time to meet with a worship pastor or worship leader to plan the upcoming week's service.

In this chapter, we will present a best-case scenario and what a senior pastor should be striving toward in the ministry of the local church.

1. The senior pastor is a visionary leader
First and foremost, the senior pastor must lead the church in discerning God's purposes for the local congregation. It is the senior pastor's ultimate responsibility to remind the church of the "big picture" or the ultimate vision for the people of God. This connects to the first key in planning a worship service. The leadership should be able to define clearly what their pastor's vision is and what steps they are taking to accomplish that vision. The pastor should have a leadership team that can be trusted implicitly. After all, there should be opportunities for many different leaders to be involved in worship services from time to time, and there must be an established amount of trust.

Once this trust is established and the worship leader is familiar with the pastor's style and vision, then the pastor can focus on their most important role is in the worship service – the preaching and teaching of the Word of God (Acts 6:4).

2. The senior pastor is a preacher and teacher
In the desirable scenario, the role of the senior pastor in organizing a worship service includes five primary areas:

a. Yearly planning of preaching and teaching
Every pastor should prayerfully consider the practice of planning a teaching/preaching schedule in advance. The same Holy Spirit that can give you a message in the midnight hour on Saturday night is the same Holy Spirit who knows what he wants you to speak even a year in advance. This is a very important discipline that can

contribute to the church's health and development. Take a weekend at the end of every year to pray about what the LORD would want you to focus on in the year ahead. How many times do you want to take communion? When do you want to do baptisms and baby dedications? Surprisingly, this pre-planning time allows extra freedom and space for creativity. Not only can your team plan special illustrations for your messages or artistic elements in the worship service, but even Sunday school classes and Kids ministries can be ready to focus on the main theme for that Sunday or that message series. Ultimately, planning in advance allows your leadership team to contribute to the overall vision from week to week.

b. Weekly planning of preaching and teaching
At the beginning of every week, you should make time to discuss positive and negative elements of the recent service. What are the areas that can be improved? What went well?

c. Co-operation with staff
After this is discussed, begin discussing the upcoming service. What is your theme for Sunday? Are you having a baptism or baby dedication that week? Are there any specific announcements that you want mentioned? Who do you want to open service? Who do you want to do announcements or take up offering? Hopefully, many of the details of the service have already been pre-planned and are on a calendar; so, at this time, your worship pastor should be able to give you any ideas to connect with your specific theme – for example, a special skit or drama or a new song that the worship team is learning for this week's message.

d. Trust in staff
After you discuss your overall vision for the week, you must trust your worship pastor to take the reins and create the worship set list (song list) as well as the order of service. Many times, if you do not have an experienced worship pastor, you must help train and encourage them through this process. Allowing them space to learn and even make mistakes regarding how a service should flow will help build even more trust in the pastor/worship leader relationship. From time to time, you may have a specific song on your mind that you would like for the worship team to sing and you

should feel free to give your input; however, you must fight the urge to micromanage your worship leader in their role. Allow them to choose the songs and give input on the order of service. Give them space to hear from God and make a spiritual contribution to every worship experience.

e. Sermon preparation

A best practice in sermon preparation is to make a habit of having one day (preferably early in the week such as Tuesday) to prepare your sermon for Sunday. If you do not make this time a priority, something will always find its way onto your calendar to hinder you. There are times that you must go to the hospital to visit someone ill or officiate a funeral, but do not allow others to monopolize on your time. Place this dedicated time on your schedule every week. When someone asks if they can meet with you, tell them you have a previously scheduled engagement. If people just show up at your office unannounced, then find another place to go and study. This must be your top priority in preparing for Sunday. We have found that when you have most of your message outlined and ready for Sunday, then if you also teach in a midweek service, you will find it easier to prepare for that as well. Then on Thursday, you can wrap up your message and add final touches and insights. Many pastors will do a final read-through on Saturday night to make it even more familiar before service on Sunday morning.

3. The senior pastor oversees Sunday worship

On Sunday morning your role is overseer and co-facilitator. Allow each moving part to operate without supervision, trusting that each leader is fully capable of executing the task at hand. Offer support and encouragement, giving appreciation and approval to each leader and volunteer who give their time. Allow your worship leader space to facilitate the move of the Holy Spirit; and, as a team, keep an open line of communication in order to facilitate the flow of service. Many times, you may want to say something during the time of praise and worship; but work together with your worship leader, so that they can help open up space for your involvement of that time. There are also times that you may want the worship team to continue singing a song or deviate from the planned outline of service. In that scenario, you and your worship leader should have a mode of communication so that they know what you are asking for.

4. The senior pastor is a team builder

In order for your church to grow and your team to flourish, there must be a level of trust and delegation, so that you have the freedom to focus on the most important elements of your role as senior pastor. Plan ahead and work as a team to accomplish the vision that God has given you as the shepherd of your flock.

B. The role of the worship leader

Regardless of your title as worship leader, music director, or worship pastor, you must see yourself as a pastor. You are helping your pastor shepherd your team, and in many cases, you can have a greater influence and impact on the people in your team than the senior pastor can. After all, you have recruited and trained, discipled, taught and led – you have helped pastor your team.

1. The worship pastor supports the senior pastor

Your pastor has a lot to deal with and God has placed you in this role to be a supporter and an encourager to the pastor. You should look for ways on a day-to-day basis to let your pastor know that you are praying for them and you are available to assist them in what they need accomplished. Many times this means stepping outside of your job description. You are here to support the overall vision they have of the ministry and where God is leading the church. You will not always agree with their ideas or input, but in order for them to put their full trust in your leadership, you must honor their decisions and respect their direction.

2. The worship pastor protects the senior pastor

If you work side-by-side with your pastor in the office daily, you should be doing everything you can do to shield them from unwanted and unscheduled visits, helping protect the time that they need in order to get the message ready for Sunday. This might not sound like it should be part of organizing a worship service, but if from week-to-week your pastor does not get anything done in the office and has to sacrifice time with their family on the weekend to get the message together, it will affect the worship service negatively. Encourage them to close their door and focus on the message, ensuring them that you will take care of the phone and other things that come up.

3. The worship pastor plans

It is your responsibility to craft the worship experience. Look at the calendar ahead of time and start planning your worship sets (song lists). Find different leaders to open the service or end the service with prayer, and pre-plan artistic elements to support the theme or sermon series that your pastor is preaching. Maybe you allow different vocalists to sing special solos? If you do, then plan that ahead of time and schedule it. Does your pastor like to serve communion once a month? If so, schedule this in advance. You will find that when you keep up with many of these small details, the trust between you and the senior pastor will grow stronger and stronger.

a. Seasonal planning

In most cases, the worship pastor oversees all creative aspects of the worship experience. This would include special Christmas plays or cantatas, Easter celebrations, etc. You should begin planning what you want to do for Christmas in late September, and in January, you should be already thinking about Easter. Here is a special note about Christmas and Easter services: many times, we plan our Easter Sunday service and our Christmas Sunday service to be a huge production with new songs and arrangements, dramas, lights, cameras, and action. Please understand that every visitor that experiences your worship service on Easter Sunday and Christmas will come back expecting to have the same quality experience as they did the Sunday before. If you have a twenty-one piece orchestra on Easter Sunday and then, because your whole team is exhausted, you have a stripped down acoustic set with just you, a guitar, and a djembe drum the Sunday after Easter, then it is safe to say that they may never return. Always try to do your BEST AVERAGE Sunday service on days that you know the most visitors will show up.

b. Weekly planning

There should be a time that you meet with your pastor to discuss the previous worship service and what went well, but also what could use improvement. What is the theme of your pastor's message? Are you doing a baptism this week or baby dedications? You should already have an idea of what is coming based upon your calendar. You should already have planned if you are going to have a drama, skit, or some other creative element in the service. What songs are you doing this week? (Typically, if you have a band, and/or choir, and singers, you should know your set list at least a week in advance.) Who will to open the service? Who will make the announcements? Who will receive the offering? Does the pastor want someone else to close the service in prayer so that he can walk to the door to visit with people as they leave the sanctuary?

c. Volunteer scheduling

Who is playing in the band on Sunday? Who is singing? These are things you should know at least a week in advance. One tool to help you in organizing the worship experience is to use a scheduling software such as planningcenteronline.com. Planning Center leads the industry in service and volunteer planning. I would highly recommend using them or a service similar to theirs.

d. Teamwork

You and your pastor are a team whose sole purpose is to create an atmosphere for God to move and then facilitate the direction in which the Holy Spirit wants to go. Work together with your pastor in doing whatever you can to promote a steady and uninterrupted flow of service.

e. Worship set list preparation

As the worship pastor, you know how important it is to choose the right songs at the right time. Proper song selection comes first through prayer. Secondly, you must be connected to the vision or theme for the week. You do not necessarily have to choose every song to fit the sermon series or subject matter, but there should be a seamless flow of content between the music, creative arts, the message, and finally the altar song or closing song. Many worship pastors sing four or five songs every Sunday, back-to-back, with no space in between. Leading worship is not like running a race, and it is not a contest to see how many songs you can sing in twenty or thirty minutes. You MUST create space to allow God to move. You must facilitate a time where the congregation can experience God and hear his voice. Create space in your worship set.

f. Rehearsal

If you have a worship team and band; then, hopefully, you have a separate day of the week that you rehearse before service. It is very important that you set the example in being prepared for rehearsal. Rehearsal and practice are two different things. Practice is what you should be doing during the week as you are going over the songs you have chosen for Sunday. Practice is getting ready for rehearsal. You should already be familiar with the songs when you arrive to rehearse. If you set this expectation, then your team will follow your lead. There is nothing that will waste your time and everyone else's time more than a team of people that come into rehearsal unprepared and unfamiliar with the songs. This means you should already be familiar with the vocal parts and chord arrangements of your songs. Lead by example. You will find that the more prepared you are for rehearsal, the more confident you will be on Sunday, and the more confident you are, the more you can focus on worshiping. When you lack confidence, you are forced to focus more on mechanics, and it will be harder for you to be sensitive to the movement of the Holy Spirit in worship.

g. Last look

Before the end of the work week, send your final order of service to the pastor for them to look over. If there are any changes that need to be made, do them before you leave. Make sure the stage is set up for Sunday, and that you have the pastor's PowerPoint loaded into the computer along with the lyrics for all the songs for praise and worship. Make sure that before you leave the office at the end of the week, you can relax and spend time with your family. If you are well-prepared, you will also be able to have much more confidence on Sunday morning. You will know that everything has been taken care of, and everything is in order. This way, when something comes up (and it always does), you will be able to handle it with finesse.

4. The worship pastor leads worship on Sunday

Sunday is when lives are changed and the Church touches heaven. People will be impacted and newcomers will either fall in love with the Church, or they will decide not to return. You have been working toward this day all week. It is time to put your plan on the table and allow God the space to do whatever he wants, however he wants.

It is very important to remember that there are many people who walk into the church and head straight for the pastor, ready to tell them all their negative experiences from the week. The worship pastor should not add to the senior pastor's burden by complaining about the little things that are not falling into place before service. The senior pastor does not need to know, right before service starts, that your bass player did not show up, or your sound guy called in sick. Just do what you can to take care of the situation and then do your best to navigate through it. Your pastor needs staff members that will not pull on them for everything, but will take the initiative to deal with a situation when it arises. Things happen, but I guarantee that your pastor will appreciate your shielding them from knowing every little thing that might be going wrong before service. You are here to help facilitate the direction of this service.

During worship, create space for people to encounter God, and then wait for God's direction. There may be moments where you do not have direction. You may not be sure whether to keep going or to move on to the next part of the service. You and your pastor should establish a way that you communicate in these situations. Keep eye contact with the pastor in order to find out the direction that they want to go. They may tell you to keep singing. If they do, then go for it. Keep an ear open and an eye out for anything that needs your attention during the service. Be ready to jump up at a moment's notice if a microphone dies or the pulpit needs to be moved. Stay ready and alert at all times.

Conclusion

The LORD will honor your preparation. If you have prayed for God's favor and you have followed the leading of the Holy Spirit, God will manifest his presence and display his glory in the midst of the Church. People will be inspired, transformed, saved, healed, delivered, and filled with the Spirit.

(This chapter on Planning a Worship Service was contributed by Stephen R. Martin, worship pastor at the Cleveland Worship Center in Cleveland, Georgia USA).

Questions for Review and Application

1. Explain how a lifestyle of worship prepares us for Sunday worship.

2. How do we keep the focus on the worship of God?

3. List the four main roles of the senior pastor.

4. Explain how the worship pastor and senior pastor interact regarding the vision for the church.

5. List and explain the senior pastor's five elements of planning.

   (1)

   (2)

   (3)

   (4)

   (5)

6. Describe the senior pastor's role in Sunday morning worship.

7. Name some of your own ideas for team building.

8. List the four major roles of the worship leader.

9. Why is it important that the worship leader support the senior pastor?

10. Name three ways that the worship leader can protect the senior pastor.

11. List and describe the worship leader's six elements of planning.

    (1)

(2)

(3)

(4)

(5)

(6)

12. Discuss the worship leader's most important concerns and functions on Sunday morning.

Resources for Further Study

Archer, Melissa L., 'I Was in the Spirit on the LORD's Day': A Pentecostal Engagement with Worship in the Apocalypse (Cleveland, TN: CPT Press, 2015).

Boone, R. Jerome, 'Community and Worship: The Key Components of Pentecostal Christian Formation', Journal of Pentecostal Theology 8 (1996), pp. 129-42.

Lombard, John A., Jr. and Jerald J. Daffe, Spiritual Gifts: For Today? For Me? (Cleveland, TN: Pathway Press, 2008).

Martin, Lee Roy (ed.), Toward a Pentecostal Theology of Preaching (Cleveland, TN: CPT Press, 2015).

Martin, Lee Roy (ed.), Toward a Pentecostal Theology of Worship (Cleveland, TN: CPT Press, 2016).

Sterbens, Tom, "Worship: The Journey to Worth," in R. Keith Whitt and French L. Arrington (eds.), Issues in Contemporary Pentecostalism (Cleveland, TN: Pathway Press, 2012), pp. 185-210.

Thomas, John Christopher, "Toward a Pentecostal Theology of Anointed Cloths," in Lee Roy Martin (ed.), Toward a Pentecostal Theology of Worship (Cleveland, TN: CPT Press, 2016), pp. 91-113.

Towns, Elmer L., Putting an End to Worship Wars (Nashville, TN: Broadman & Holman Publishers, 1997).

Whitt, R. Keith and French L. Arrington (eds.), Issues in Contemporary Pentecostalism (Cleveland, TN: Pathway Press, 2012).

Made in the USA
Lexington, KY
10 December 2017